W9-BTA-383

THE BOOK OF WICCA

THE BOOK
OF WICCA

Bring love, healing, and harmony into your life
with the power of natural magic

LUCY SUMMERS

A QUARTO BOOK

Copyright © 2001 Quarto Inc.

First edition for the United States, its territories and
dependencies, and Canada published in 2001 by
Barron's Educational Series, Inc.

All rights reserved. No part of this book may be reproduced
in any form, by photostat, microfilm, xerography, or any
other means, or incorporated into any information retrieval
system, electronic or mechanical, without the written
permission of the copyright owner.

All inquiries should be addressed to:
Barron's Educational Series, Inc.
250 Wireless Boulevard
Hauppauge, NY 11788
http://www.barronseduc.com

Library of Congress Catalog Card Number: 00-110924

International Standard Book Number: 0-7641-5400-1

Conceived, designed, and produced by
Quarto Publishing plc
The Old Brewery
6 Blundell Street
London N7 9BH

QUAR: WICC

Senior editor: Michelle Pickering
Senior art editor: Sally Bond
Assistant art director: Penny Cobb
Designer: Heather Blagden
Photographer: Michael Wicks
Illustrator: Judy Stevens
Picture research: Image Select International
Indexer: Dorothy Frame

Art director: Moira Clinch
Publisher: Piers Spence

Manufactured by Regent Publishing Services Ltd, Hong Kong
Printed by Midas Printing Ltd, China

9 8 7 6 5 4 3 2 1

WARNING

Working with candles and burning
incense can be hazardous. The author,
publisher, and copyright holder
assume no responsibility for any
injury or damage caused or sustained
while performing any of the rites and
spells outlined in this book. Check
that any candles you buy do not
contain lead wicks before purchasing.

AUTHOR'S NOTE

The words spoken in the rituals in
this book are from my own Book of
Shadows, and follow the Gardnerian/
Alexandrian tradition. You will find
different words used in different
books and traditions, but their
essence remains the same. Similarly,
the order in which circlework is
practiced may also change, except
for casting the circle, invoking the
elements, and closing the circle.
It is perfectly acceptable to adapt the
content and order of the remaining
components to suit your own needs.

contents

INTRODUCTION

Wicca—the ancient religion of Witchcraft—has become extremely popular in recent years as people seek to establish a connection with the natural world. Many people find that the individualism and joyful nature of Wicca can help to fill the emptiness that modern life can bring; it draws us closer to nature, each other, and ourselves.

Above: Elizabeth Sawyer was executed as a Witch in England in 1621. Although Witchcraft was severely threatened by the Christian authorities for many centuries, it has now risen in popularity once more and is known as both Witchcraft and Wicca.

The past century's relentless march of progress has done much to divorce us from the rhythms and cycles of nature; the Wiccan way of life attempts to redress this imbalance by celebrating the seasons, working with nature, and rediscovering the rites of passage within our lives. Nondogmatic, nurturing, and empowering, Wicca can provide an alternative way of life that enables us to grow as people as well as maintain respect for the earth on which we live.

Witchcraft is a traditional nature religion, and is closely linked with the paganism of our ancestors. Many people think of Witchcraft as a thing of the past, but in fact it has never ceased to exist. Christianity may have suppressed Witchcraft, but it failed to eradicate it. However, it was not until the repeal of the Witchcraft Act in Britain in 1951 that Wicca really came to the fore once more. Gerald B. Gardner was one of the first Witches to acknowlege his beliefs publicly, writing a "Book of Shadows" detailing Wiccan rituals and spells that generated

Left: The publications of Gerald B. Gardner in the 1950s helped to popularize Wicca.

a great deal of interest. Within twenty years, the number of people drawn to Wicca had grown enormously; it became popular worldwide, finding a strong base in the United States and Australia as well as reemerging in Germany, France, and the Baltic states. Maxine and Alex Sanders became leading exponents, and began the tradition known as Alexandrian Wicca, though in fact it differed little from Gardnerian Wicca. Many other traditions were established over the following years, such as Dianic Wicca, Celtic Wicca, Seax Wicca, and the Kingstone Tradition. Some are based on similar principles to Gardnerian/Alexandrian Wicca, while others have developed along separate paths. Due to its nondogmatic and individualistic nature, Wicca is now a mixture of many ways of working, often varying from coven to coven and from person to person. This book is a guide to its general principles.

Right: Doreen Valiente, Gerald Gardner's high priestess, wrote some beautiful ritual pieces, including "The Charge," the invocation used by many Wiccans during the drawing down the moon ritual (see pages 66–67).

PRINCIPLES OF WICCA

Wicca may be a very individualistic religion, but
there are some aspects that remain constant. All
Wiccans respect nature, both animate and inanimate;
seek connection with the divine creative forces,
in the form of the Goddess and God; and believe in
a positive morality that emphasizes responsibility
for personal actions and self-development.

QUESTIONS AND ANSWERS

The basic principles of Wicca are outlined here in the form of answers to questions that are commonly asked, both by people who are interested in embracing the Wiccan way of life as well as by those who fear it because it is the unknown.

WHAT DOES THE WORD "WICCA" MEAN?

Wicca comes from the Old English for "Witch." It is also related to the Middle Low German word "wicken," meaning "to conjure," to the Swedish "vicka," meaning "to move to and fro," and to the Icelandic word "vitki," from the verb "to know." The word reflects the magical nature of the religion of Wicca.

WHAT DO WICCANS DO?

Wiccans have an intimate connection with nature and seasonal rhythms, which they celebrate with festivals to mark certain points in the agricultural calendar, such as springtime and harvest. There are eight seasonal festivals, known as sabbats. Rituals are also held at other times of year, usually during a full moon. These are known as esbats, and may be held simply to celebrate the full moon or for nonseasonal festivities such as a handfasting (the term used for a Wiccan marriage). Sometimes sabbats and esbats are simply celebratory; at other times magic or healings are performed. Wiccan rituals are held within the sacred confines of a magic circle.

Yin/yang symbol.

WHAT DO WICCANS BELIEVE IN?

Wiccans believe in a force or energy that flows through all life and connects everything. They worship this energy in the form of the Goddess and God—the female and male aspects of creation. The Goddess and God play an important part in the life of a Witch. They are worshiped in many different forms and under many different names, each representing an aspect of male and female divinity. They are to be found everywhere in the natural world, in trees, plants, rivers, springs, rocks, stars, the sun, the moon, as well as in ourselves.

Unlike many of today's orthodox religions, the Goddess has an equal standing with her male counterpart, and within Wicca, women are more than respected and revered as her priestesses and the carriers of life. The God and Goddess can be seen as two complementary halves of a whole, each possessing different attributes and powers that fit together seamlessly to represent the whole of life and nature. In essence, it is similar to the Taoist belief in yin and yang, the complementary but opposite aspects of the "life breath" they call chi.

Above: Wicca is a spiritual path whose main focus is to become more in tune with the natural world and thereby achieve a balanced and productive life. To do this, Wiccans celebrate eight main annual festivals that mark the seasonal rhythms of nature.

Far left: Wiccans worship a God and Goddess, whom they regard as the two aspects of a universal life force, similar to the yin and yang aspects of chi energy in Taoism.

THE GODDESS

Right: Wiccans often revere the Goddess in the form of Diana, mistress of the moon and hunting.

The Goddess has myriad names and faces, and lives in every corner of the earth. She is usually represented in her three phases of life: as maiden, mother, and crone. As maiden, she represents innocence and purity, all hopes as yet unfulfilled. The Romans worshiped her as Diana, the Greeks as Artemis. As mother, she appears with the full moon. With a child in her belly, she safeguards the hearth of her people. The Egyptians worshiped her as Isis, the Greeks as Demeter. The crone aspect of the Goddess encompasses all that is wise. She is the wielder of magic, the dark side of the moon; she is not always benign. Of all aspects it is the crone who walks closest to death and rebirth; it is she, worshiped as Hecate by the Greeks, who knows the other realms.

The Goddess also wears other masks, including that of warrior, traveler, and lover. She is in all women and all women are in the Goddess. She understands every joy and pain, every struggle and triumph of womanhood, and provides a light in the darkness to all those who seek to know that they are in no way inferior to anyone else on earth.

THE GOD

The God is usually represented as either the lover or son of the Goddess. His attributes are strength, justice, protection, and the guardianship of all things wild. He stands sentry at the doorway between life and death. Most Witches see the God as the Greek Pan or British Herne, lords of the hunt, resplendent with horns. Early Christians demonized Pan's image, borrowing his cloven hooves and horns for their devil, Satan. In fact, the Bible never describes Satan as having such an appearance.

In some Wiccan traditions, harvest is the time when the God dies in order to fertilize the Goddess. He is then reborn with the Winter Solstice when the sun is reborn. Other traditions regard winter as the God's time of year and summer as the time of the Goddess. Some regard the whole year as a continuous dance between the two deities.

Above: The God is frequently depicted as Pan, lord of the hunt and guardian of nature.

WHAT IS THE DIFFERENCE BETWEEN WICCANS AND WITCHES?

There is no difference, so you will find that both terms are used interchangeably throughout this book. With a few exceptions, most initiated Wiccans also refer to themselves, proudly, as Witches. Those reticent to do so are often worried that the term Witch still carries too many negative connotations to be acceptable in the modern age. Fairy tales have a lot to answer for.

DO WICCANS CAST SPELLS?

Wiccans use spells to heal and help, but have an ethic never to harm. Mostly Wiccans see enough magic in their everyday lives—the birth of a baby, the bursting of leaf buds on a tree, a beautiful sunset—that they do not need to use spells to make themselves more attractive, rich, powerful, and so on. Somehow, being aware that you have the

power to cast magic spells makes you less likely to use them. That is all part of the magic.

Witches also practice many of the divinatory arts—the tarot, casting runestones, scrying with crystal balls or mirrors; they frequently do not use them to see the future but to help them counsel someone who comes to them for advice instead. In this way, most Witches develop a feel for lay psychology. Knowing how the human mind works is, in itself, a doorway to a powerful kind of healing magic.

ARE THERE WHITE WITCHES AND BLACK WITCHES?

Most Witches prefer not to be labeled either a white Witch or a black Witch. Being a Wiccan means that you stand by Wiccan ethics and respect all nature; doing anything that may be harmful— that is, on the "black" side—can have nothing to do with Wicca. The labels white Witch and black Witch are therefore meaningless, since all Wiccan magic should be done for the purposes of good. However, all faiths, including Wicca, have their dubious practitioners.

WHAT IS A COVEN?

A coven is a group of Witches who meet regularly for ritual occasions. The traditional number of a coven is thirteen, consisting of roughly equal numbers of men and women. In reality, most covens are smaller than this, and the numbers of men and women are often unbalanced. The coven is led by a high priestess and a high priest, who are assisted by a coven maiden (usually a young unmarried woman with a couple of years' ritual experience). In some traditions the coven is nonhierarchical, and different members take on the role of priest, priestess, and maiden each month. Being a member of a coven usually requires initiation of some kind.

Above: The five-pointed pentagram is a major symbol of Witchcraft.

Below: Traditionally, there are thirteen Witches in a coven, but in reality most are smaller than this.

WHAT IS A SOLITARY?

A solitary is a Wiccan who chooses or perhaps has no choice but to work alone. There are many solitaries and they all have their own way of working. Some Wiccans maintain that working in a group or coven is better because you get more training, and because it is more difficult to get deluded by your imagination and ego. Some also feel that it is safer. While all of the above may be true, it is not necessarily the case all the time. Not all covens have leaders who are well trained in the arts of Wicca and magic, and some covens are full of people with egos and delusions. Covens can also get mired down from time to time in coven politics, whether internal or external, which can be a frustrating distraction.

Solitaries, on the other hand, can work at their own pace and in their own way, and the learning can often be more profound. The greatest problem with working on a solitary path is loneliness; many Wiccans who work on their own lament that they have no one to ask questions of if they are unsure about anything, or generally talk to about their beliefs.

Above: A solitary is a Witch who practices Wicca on his or her own. This may be by choice or because there is no coven nearby to join.

HOW DO YOU BECOME A WICCAN?

An initation rite is usually performed. Initiation is like a threshold for the spirit to cross before it can attain a new level on its path of learning. Ritual initiations are performed by covens to serve a dual purpose: to bond the members of the coven together and to alter the mind-set of the initiate so that he or she can move onto another stage of development. Often there is more than one initiation, although they are spread out over time. These represent different levels that the initiate has reached. In Gardnerian/Alexandrian Wicca, for example, there are three levels of initiation: the first degree making you a priest or priestess and Witch; the second degree making you a high priest or priestess, with the right to initiate others and conduct ceremonies; and

the third degree, giving you the right to run your own coven independently. Of course, most covens will not initiate a new member to first degree without a certain amount of training. This is usually done by means of a period of training in an outer circle that exists outside the magic circle within which the initiates perform their rituals.

Solitaries may wish to self-initiate. A self-initiation ritual is described on pages 92–93, and there are plenty of rituals to be found in other books. For example, Doreen Valiente's *Witchcraft for Tomorrow* has a good self-initiation rite in it. Or if you wish, you may construct your own, or simply offer a prayer of dedication to the God and Goddess, asking them to help you on your way. There is no right or wrong way; as with most things in Wicca, what works for you is right. However, bear in mind that Wicca, or for that matter any spiritual path, cannot be learned in a month, a year, or even a couple of years; it is a lifetime's journey. Initiations and degrees in themselves do not make you wise, or even a true Wiccan.

Above: Initiated Wiccans wear a cord around the waist, often blue for a man and red for a woman.

Left: Candles provide illumination, ambience, and represent the element fire during rituals.

IS WICCA A WAY OF LIFE?

Of course. Any initiate can turn up the required number of times a year, know the words by heart, then go home and spend the time until the next occasion eating fast-food and slumped in front of the television. Wicca is not just about what you know, but about who you are and what you do on this planet.

Wicca is in essence a nature religion, so Witches have a deep respect for the natural world and a sense of the role they play in its conservation or destruction. We live on a beautiful and diverse earth, one that provides us with all we need to live and thrive. Not only us, but also all the animals, birds, trees, fish, reptiles, and plants. The more we discover about the world around us, the more we realize how everything fits together like a complex jigsaw puzzle in which every single piece is essential. Remove one piece and the picture starts to become distorted; remove too many and it is lost altogether.

Wicca provides a sound basis for thinking about environmental topics. Most Wiccans try to leave as light a footprint on the earth as possible, recycling everything they can, conserving energy, and taking part in projects to improve their local area. Some covens regularly take trips to local places of natural beauty and clear up after thoughtless day-trippers and picnickers. They may also spend time in prayer and meditation, sending healing and love to the earth and the trees. Whatever we do on this earth, what matters is that we try to be good guardians so that in turn our children can enjoy the world and continue to care for it.

WHAT IS THE "WICCAN REDE"?

The Wiccan Rede is the basic law of ethics of the Wiccan faith. The most frequently quoted portion is:

Eight words the
Wiccan Rede fulfill
An' it harm none
Do what you will

This means that you can do whatever you want in life, but make sure that your actions do not cause harm to others.

Above and far left: Wiccans try to help conserve the earth's beauty and minimize the detrimental effect that humanity often has on the environment.

WHY DO WICCANS WORK MANY OF THEIR RITUALS AT NIGHT?

It is really a question of tradition. When Witchcraft was still illegal, it was safer to work at night because there were fewer people about, and this habit has continued to the present day. Another reason is that most people are busy with some kind of work in the daytime. Night is also the realm of the moon aspect of the Goddess, so it is the ideal time in which to work her rites. However, although most rituals are still performed at night, some are celebrated during the day, such as Wiccanings and handfastings (see pages 91 and 94).

DO WICCANS WORK NAKED?

There are some Witches and covens that prefer to work naked, or skyclad as it is otherwise known. However, the majority wear some kind of robes or special clothes. Neither way of working is wrong as long as the individual is happy and relaxed with it. Skyclad Wiccans maintain that they work naked so that all appear equal. Some also claim that magical power is more easily raised without clothing. However, the opposite camp maintains that a piece of material is no obstacle to raising power. Of course, both have their disadvantages: being skyclad can be extremely chilly in cold climates, and robes can be rather risky when working around a fire.

IS THERE ANY SEX INVOLVED?

Wicca, along with many nature-based religions, has an unashamed view of sex. This does not mean that it condones any harmful or illegal sexual practices; it certainly does not. Although much sexual imagery is used—for example, in blessing the wine (see page 63)—sexual intercourse within a ritual is uncommon. When it does happen, in a ceremony called the Great Rite, it usually takes place between established couples and in private. Some covens incorporate sexual initiation as part of the third degree rite, but on the whole it is only carried out in token. Consent must always be given. In truth, most Wiccans have never been part of or witnessed sex taking place within a ritual.

Above: Wiccans either wear robes or work naked, which is known as skyclad.

Right: Rituals are often performed at night because of tradition and the fact that most people have to work during the day. Night is also the realm of the moon aspect of the Goddess.

WHAT IS THE DIFFERENCE BETWEEN A PAGAN AND A WICCAN?

Both are spiritual paths that follow a nature tradition, and apart from the labels, there is not a great deal of difference between them these days. One might argue that Wicca contains more magical rituals and has a tighter structure, whereas paganism is more eclectic and "lighter" in content. In addition, many pagans would not want to be considered Wiccans, because they see it as a completely separate path, complete with initiations.

Above: Paganism and Wicca are very similar. Both revere nature and celebrate its seasons.

DO WICCANS WORSHIP SATAN?

No. Satan is part and parcel of the Christian religion, so to worship him, Wiccans would have to believe in Christianity. Christians often describe Satan as a horned god, which many in the past have confused with the Wiccan God as represented by Pan or Herne, both of whom are depicted with horns. In fact, the Christian religion took the image of the horned god of ancient fertility religions and superimposed its idea of Satan over him. The Bible, however, contains no descriptions of Satan's appearance.

DO WICCANS HAVE FAMILIARS?

Familiars are Witches' pets that are supposed to help Witches with their magic, or to possess supernatural powers themselves. Many Wiccans do indeed keep an animal as a companion, and some of these could be regarded as familiars in the traditional sense. However, while some

Left: Early 20th-century Witches conducting a divination seance in Brittany, France. In the past, people often confused the magical powers of Witches with the powers of Satan, though in reality there is no connection whatsoever.

domestic animals love being part of rituals, others prefer to find a quiet corner, curl up, and have a good sleep instead.

Left: A black cat is a traditional Witch's familiar.

TOOLS OF THE CRAFT

Witches use magical tools in their rituals to summon
spirits, invoke deities, and to consecrate and bless.
From the sword to the bell, each tool is lovingly
cherished and is never used for non-magical purposes.
Whether handmade or bought, each one will last
the lifetime of the Witch … and beyond.

MAGICAL TOOLS

The use of tools for ritual purposes is not confined to Wicca. In fact, most major religions use objects when conducting their ceremonies. Altars, wands, and incense are fairly universal, whereas special cords and pentacles are not so common.

Wiccan tools are used to direct energy according to the Witch's will. It must be remembered that the tools, although consecrated for ritual use (see page 60), have no power in themselves—they act merely as a focus for your own power. It follows, then, that tools are less important to a ritual than your own inner power, although they certainly enhance a ritual.

Above and right: Special tools are used in most religions, including Christianity. Wiccan tools must be cleansed in water or earth before ritual use.

Magical tools can be acquired in a number of ways. They can be handed down through members of a coven or family, made, or bought. If you have a practical and creative nature, making tools is the best option because the finished product will become enhanced with your own powers. Junk stores are a fun way to find other tools. White-handled knives and chalices can often be found from such sources. If you are unable to find a magical tool, do not let it stop you from practicing Wicca; improvise instead. Remember that there is no right or wrong way to perform a ritual, and that your inner power is all that is truly needed.

CLEANSING TOOLS

If a tool has come from an unknown source, such as via a junk store, it is best to cleanse it. Either place it in salt water, in running water (a stream or small waterfall is best, but make sure the tool is tied securely in place so that it does not wash away), or bury it in the earth. Cleanse tools during a full moon, leaving them in place overnight. The tool will still need to be consecrated before ritual use (see page 60).

SWORD

The sword symbolizes control, strength, honor, and nobility. The magical sword is not used to kill or injure; in fact, it is not used for any operation that is not magical. Representing the male principle, it is the weapon of the element fire. The sword is used during the ritual for casting the magic circle within which Wiccan ceremonies are performed, as well as to challenge any malevolent spirits. The power of the sword protects those within the circle. Swords can be purchased from militaria stores and at historical reenactment fairs, but an athame can be used in its place if a sword is not available; some traditions never use a sword.

AThAME

Pronounced ath-ay-me, this black-handled, blunt-bladed knife is a Witch's most personal tool. Each Witch should have his or her own athame, and no other Witch should use it. In some covens, a period of training must be undergone before a Witch acquires an athame. Magically it can be thought of as a smaller representation of the sword, able to carry out any operation the sword can do. This is useful if working alone or in a small coven, as a sword can be hard to find or may be impractical to use. An athame can be home-produced or bought; if the latter, you will probably have to buy a sharp knife and blunt the blade yourself.

The athame is carried in a sheath, which can be made from two shaped pieces of leather sewn together, and hung on a cord around the waist. The knife is often inscribed or painted with magical sigils (pictured on the right), usually on the hilt but sometimes on the blade.

WHITE-HANDLED KNIFE

This is the Witch's "practical" knife, used for any tasks that would not be suitable for the sword or athame. This includes cutting ritual food and inscribing sigils into candles for candle magic. As with the athame, the white-handled knife can be purchased, although a beautiful knife can be made at home from an old blade and a piece of wood or bone for the hilt.

Male	Female
God	
Initial of the God	
Scourge	
Kiss	

Power of the athame

Breasts of the Goddess

Initial of the Goddess

The world

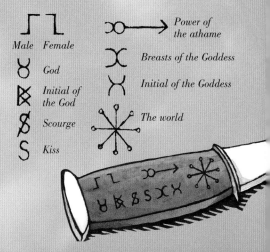

ALTAR

The altar provides the focus within the magic circle for the ritual. Usually adorned by statues or other representations of the God and Goddess, Wiccan altars are often masterpieces of art in their own right; some are handcrafted using five different types of wood. However, in reality any table or chest can be used; a chest has the added advantage of providing a storage space for the magical tools when not in use. Altars are usually covered with a cloth, kept specially for this purpose, which can be any color and either plain or decorated.

A Wiccan altar usually has upon it two altar candles, a candle for the cardinal point north, dishes of salt and water, a censer, pentacle, white-handled knife, chalice, wand, scourge, and bell. The sword is placed on the floor in front of the altar, and a cauldron, together with any sabbat cakes and unconsecrated wine, at the side of the altar until required for use. In addition, sweet-scented flowers, fruits, vegetables, crystals, pebbles, and driftwood are often used to adorn the altar.

Many Wiccans maintain their own personal, daily altar, often set up in a quiet corner of the house. It tends to be adorned with a more eclectic collection of symbols and objects that matter to the person.

CHALICE

The cup or goblet that is used to hold the sacred red wine or other liquid that is drunk during a ritual is called the chalice. Most often it is in the form of a pottery or metallic goblet, without handles; some Wiccans use wooden chalices. It is inadvisable to use cheap metal or even silver, as red wine causes a reaction that can lead to bad-tasting wine and a discolored chalice. The chalice symbolizes the feminine principle, its womblike cup holding the sacred blood of life.

CANDLES

The minimum number of candles used in a ritual circle is six: two for the altar and one for each of the cardinal points. Generally, white candles are used unless a ritual or spell is being performed that requires a different color; candles used to celebrate the eight sabbats (see pages 72–89) may be of an associated color, for example. Make sure that the candles are long enough to last throughout the whole ritual, and use fresh ones each time. Take care that they are positioned safely in stable candleholders and out of strong drafts, especially if they are on the floor.

WAND

Just as the sword or athame is used to call up and control certain powers, the wand is also used to summon beings, although in a gentler way. For example, to invoke the power of the Goddess into the high priestess (see drawing down the moon, pages 66–67), you would use the wand since it would be presumptuous to summon or command the Goddess, whereas to summon the elements or the lords of the watchtowers (see pages 56–59), you would use the sword or athame.

MAKING A WAND

Wands are usually homemade, or more correctly, nature-made. A wand is traditionally cut from the first year's growth (the straighter the better) of hazel at sunrise during a new moon. It is usually about 2 feet (60cm) long. Before cutting it, ask permission from the tree and leave behind a small offering of thanks, such as a pinch of tobacco or a hair from your head. You can then prepare and decorate the wand according to your own taste. Usually, Wiccans strip the bark, leave the wood beneath to dry, and then polish it, before carving symbols into it. Some Wiccans attach a pinecone or acorn-shaped item to the tip of the wand to emphasize its phallic nature; others bind a crystal there instead, to concentrate the energy.

CENSER

This is used to hold incense and carry it around the circle when required. It is therefore preferable to have a censer with a long chain attached to the receptacle, although some Wiccans like to use a dish or shell. It is also advisable to have some kind of stand on which to place the hot censer in order to avoid burning the altar cloth.

RECIPE FOR INCENSE

2 parts frankincense
1 part myrrh
1 part sandalwood
or cedarwood
¼ part benzoin
¼ part dried rosemary
¼ part juniper berries

Mix the ingredients together and store in a cool, dry place. Burn on charcoal blocks.

INCENSE

Although some people use incense cones or sticks, most Wiccans prefer solid incense, the type burned on charcoal blocks. As with the censer, this type of incense can generally be bought in religious or New Age stores. It comes in a range of heavily scented mixtures, usually containing frankincense. Some Wiccans make their own, buying gums, herbs, and resins in bulk and mixing them according to various recipes.

PENTACLE

This is an object, usually wood, metal, or wax, onto which a pentagram is inscribed. The pentagram is a five-pointed star and a major symbol of Wicca. It represents the element earth, and the five points also symbolize the elements earth, water, air, fire, and spirit. The pentagram is usually drawn with one arm pointing upward, representing the supremacy of spirit over the elements. When reversed, it symbolizes the rulership of matter over spirit.

CAULDRON

The traditional cooking and mixing pot of Witches is these days rarely more than a decorative extra in the circle. Made of metal or pottery and having three legs, to represent the triple aspects of the Goddess, it symbolizes the element water and is associated with rebirth and inspiration. During seasonal festivals it is variously used to hold a candle, water, or flowers. It is also popular for apple-bobbing at Samhain.

BROOM

A broom is used to sweep the area where the magic circle is to be cast in order to remove any negativity before a ritual. A natural besom is ideal, but an ordinary household one will do. After use, it is usually placed out of the circle, perhaps leaning against a wall of the room.

SCOURGE

This tends to be a feature of Gardnerian/Alexandrian covens, but most Wiccans choose not to use a scourge because of its sadomasochistic overtones. In fact, it should never be used to hurt, and its thongs should be soft. The scourge has two purposes. One is to ask forgiveness of the Goddess for a wrongdoing, in which case the penitent is gently scourged three times while crouching down with his or her forehead on the pentacle. Its other use is to send the Witch into a light trance due to the rhythm of the scourge strokes.

MAKING A ROBE

You will need a piece of fabric roughly twice as long as your height and wide enough to stretch from hand to hand with your arms outstretched. Fold the fabric in half widthwise, then cut out a half-circle at the center of the folded edge to create a neck hole. Carefully cut the remaining fabric into a T shape that will loosely fit your arms and body. Sew the underarm and side edges of the fabric together, then hem the neck, wrists, and bottom of the robe. You may wish to embroider your robe with decoration.

ROBES

Some Witches prefer to work naked, or skyclad. Others choose to wear robes. Color is usually a matter of individual or group preference; by no means is black *de rigueur*, though beware of light colors because of red wine stains. Most fabrics are also acceptable, but natural fibers are preferred. Be very careful around candles and bonfires if the material you use is not fireproof.

CORDS

Most Witches own a full set of nine cords but rarely use them all. The colors and their meanings vary from tradition to tradition. In one common color system, male Wiccans wear a blue cord (east) around the waist; females wear a red cord (south). The other colors are green (west), yellow (north), purple (the circle), gold (the sun), silver (the moon), white (the ladder of the Goddess; this cord is sometimes used to measure and draw the magic circle), and black (the Goddess in her crone aspect). Traditionally, all cords should be 9 feet (3m) long, equaling the diameter of the magic circle, and have both ends sealed to prevent fraying.

Unworn cords are not generally brought into the circle unless a ritual is being performed that involves their use, such as knot magic, which involves putting knots into the cord (often a fresh one designated for the purpose) while reciting a chant that locks the spell into each knot. The cord is then buried or put away for a period of time to allow the spell to work.

BELL

Bells are used to herald the beginning and end of a ritual. A symbol of the Goddess, its notes seem to vibrate from this plane to the next, creating a positive energy around the circle.

CIRCLEWORK

All Witches and covens have their own way of
carrying out rituals. However, it is important to start
out with a good foundation, including how to cast a
circle, how to raise power within it, and how to close
the circle when the ritual is finished. Although the
specific words used may differ between traditions,
the circlework described in this chapter is standard
practice within mainstream Wicca.

DEVELOPING
A MAGICAL MIND

Spells and rituals do not work because the words spoken contain power, or because the materials used have any magic of their own. These are just props, designed to focus the mind on its purpose. The truth is that the power is within you, in your mind.

Unless you are able to slip into the right state of mind, you will not be able to work magic. It does not matter how much magical knowledge or degres of initiation you possess; these are no good without the focus of intent. In fact, there are people who may never have heard of Wicca, or even believe in magic, but who are nevertheless able to encourage things to happen through the force of their will and positive thinking.

To work magic, the mind needs to be relaxed, yet capable of thinking clearly. This state corresponds with what is known in science as the alpha brainwave pattern. This is the state your mind is in before sleep. It can be enhanced by meditation, visualization techniques, and even daydreaming.

Deeper trancework, used for divination and journeying to spirit realms, relies on a much slower brainwave pattern, known as theta. Theta patterns are found in people during deep sleep, or under anesthesia. Achieving theta patterns when awake helps to increase creativity and psychic awareness, but also makes communication more difficult. Ways of reaching a wakeful theta state include drumming, focusing on a candle flame, and listening to certain "mathematical" music, such as that produced by Bach.

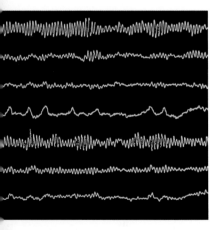

Above: Relaxing the mind into an alpha or theta brainwave pattern is ideal for working magic.

Right: Visualization techniques involve holding an attractive image in your mind in order to achieve a magical mind-set.

MEDITATION

Meditation helps to produce a deep alpha state, relaxing the mind and giving it a refreshing vacation from everyday stresses and strains. The daily practice of meditation also prepares the mind to work magic more easily. Meditation, like Wicca, has many paths and traditions, and you must find the one most suited to you. You may be happiest chanting eastern mantras, or you may prefer to concentrate on your breathing, or to open and close your chakras (inner energy centers). Some people like to use items such as candles to aid concentration, others find them distracting. Whatever method you choose, try to meditate every day, preferably at the same time.

Make sure that you will not be interrupted (switch the phone off) and settle yourself in a comfortable sitting position, either on the floor or a chair. It is best not to lie down as this makes it too easy to fall asleep. Meditate for as long as is comfortable. You may find that this is not long to begin with, but the length of time will increase the more you do it.

Above: Meditation will help you achieve a deep alpha state, ideal for circlework and other rituals.

Right: Controlling your breathing will help relax and calm you.

BREATH MEDITATION

With your eyes closed, breathe in slowly and deeply from your abdomen. At the top of the breath, hold it for a few seconds before slowly exhaling. Once you have exhaled fully, hold for a few seconds before breathing in again. Do this for at least ten cycles to begin with. This exercise has a very calming effect and is beneficial to the physical body as well as the mind.

DRUM MEDITATION

Meditating to the repetitive beating of a drum produces vibrations that send the brain into a trancelike, theta state. This has long been known in Shamanistic traditions. The Shamans of Siberia (where the term Shaman comes from) thought of their drums as horses that could carry them to other worlds. Native American traditions use the drum in the same way; it is a necessary accessory to journeying in other realms. Drum meditation is not recommended for beginners and should never be undertaken alone.

Right: Shamans use drumming to induce a trancelike, theta state before journeying to other realms.

Visualization

Visualization is the art of
being able to experience something in
your mind; not just to see it, but also to hear,
touch, smell, and taste it. Some people are naturals at
visualization, but others have to practice regularly before
they are able to hold a clear image in their heads. It is rather
like daydreaming, only more vividly and with more focus. Regular
practice at visualization also helps to strengthen the imaginative
process, leading to greater creativity.

Magically, visualization is important because when working a ritual
or a spell, you need to visualize what you wish as the outcome. You will
need to visualize it strongly, strong enough to believe in. Take away the words
and the props and this is basically what magic is—using your will and
force of imagination to influence the energies around you, so that your
desire becomes possible.

Like meditation, try to practice visualization every day, but do not
expect miracles. Everyone learns and develops these skills at their
own speed; just relax and be comfortable with it rather than forcing
yourself to attain a certain level. Visualization can be tiring,
so ground yourself afterward in the same way as you would
at the end of a ritual (see page 68).

FLOWER VISUALIZATION

This visualization takes a
week to do. Sit comfortably, as for
meditation, and make sure that you will not
be disturbed. On the first day, picture a flower in
front of you, perhaps a rose or a daisy. Picture it as a
vivid red color. See every petal and stamen. Feel its texture
and smell its perfume. Hold it in your mind as long as possible.
On the second day, do the same, but this time picture
an orange flower. As before, hold it in your mind as long as you
can. Repeat on the third day with a yellow flower, on the fourth day
with a green flower, on the fifth day with a blue flower, on the sixth
day with an indigo flower, and on the seventh day imagine a flower
that is bright white and shines with a radiant light.
Once you have mastered the individual flowers, you may like
to try visualizing them all growing in a row in front of you.
Once you have them clearly in your mind, imagine their
colors flying upward, like a rainbow, which then arches
over and bathes you in its beautiful light.

PLANNING
A RITUAL

Rituals vary from one time to the next. For example, a ritual to celebrate Beltane one year may be held in a new location the next year that results in very different energies being raised.

There is nothing wrong with tailoring a ritual to suit your own needs. Books of Shadows and rituals written in books such as this are only guidelines. The important thing about performing a ritual is that you have intent and purpose. To raise power with nowhere for it to go is more a measure of an immature ego than an accomplished Witch. The purpose may be to celebrate a festival, a full moon, to do spellwork, or a healing. Whatever it is, the person conducting the ritual must keep the purpose clear at all times and be responsible for what happens.

Rituals may take place outside or in. Many Wiccans prefer to work outside because they feel closer to nature. However, outside rituals are dependent on the weather and privacy. Obviously, those in warmer climes will be able to work outside all year round, provided they have a suitable location. In colder climates, shivering can be very distracting, and it is frustrating trying to keep candles alight in wind and rain. Privacy is also important; you do not want to start a ritual and have a crowd gather around, or to have the fire department arrive to put out your bonfire.

PHASES OF THE MOON

When planning a ceremony, the phase of the moon is always taken into account. The moon is the symbol of the mother aspect of the Goddess, the bringer of fertility and inspiration, the ruler of tides and women's cycles. She is a light in the darkness and the opener of the third eye. Mysterious and beautiful, she has held the attention and worship of mankind for millennia. Today, Wiccans still see the moon as a celestial symbol of the Goddess, her various phases bringing different energies to magical workings.

THE MOON AND ITS ASSOCIATIONS

New moon *The time of new beginnings, the seed time when ideas start to form.*

Waxing moon *The maiden aspect of the Goddess. A good time for any kind of positive magic or ritual.*

Full moon *The mother aspect of the Goddess. A time of fulfillment, blessing, and celebration. Psychic power is at its greatest.*

Waning moon *The crone aspect of the Goddess. A time for banishing magic and binding.*

The circle is a symbolic shape that has been used for magical purposes throughout the world since ancient times. It has many different meanings and functions, all of which can be used in the practice of Wicca by a group, a couple, or a person working alone.

The circumference of the circle separates that which is within from that which is without. It also has no beginning and no end, and so represents eternity. The area within the circle's edge is considered to be a place outside ordinary space and time, and indeed, rituals held within circles do often seem to take on time structures of their own, with hours of "ordinary" time rushing by in what seems like an instant. Outside of the circle ordinary time and reality exist, and to jump between the two (if really necessary) requires a little ritual of its own in order to keep the two worlds separate in everyone's mind. For magical purposes, circles are primarily used to keep out unwanted influences and to contain any power raised for magical working. In this way, the power raised can be focused for its intended purpose before sending it beyond the boundaries. It has been speculated that the stone circles found in various parts of the world were used for this purpose. They seem to be built on specific earth power lines (ley lines), and perhaps they catch the earth power and store it within their stony circumference, rather like a dam.

THE MAGIC CIRCLE

Left: Circles and five-pointed stars (pentagrams) are found in nature and therefore have special significance for Wiccans.

Right: Wiccans perform their rituals within the protective and sacred boundary of a magic circle. Ancient stone circles, such as this one in Ballynoe, County Down, in Ireland, may have been used for similar purposes.

CASTING A CIRCLE

Clear the space intended for use
and mark out a circle on the floor.
Traditionally, this should be 9 feet (3m) in diameter,
but any size that suits can be used. Mark it with something
that can be cleaned away afterward: flour, salt, chalk, or even
boughs and flowers of the season. Lay out your altar in the north of the
circle (see page 33) and place a candle at the four cardinal points. Ideally,
all objects should fit inside this marked-out circle, but if space is severely
limited, you can place things just outside it as long as you include them in the
magical sword-drawn circle later in this ritual (see page 54); always remember
that you can adapt Wiccan rituals and practices to suit your own needs.

SWEEPING THE CIRCLE

Take the broom and sweep the circle from the middle out to the edges in a deosil
(sunwise, or clockwise) manner. If you like, you may chant a little rune such as:

Sweep, sweep, sweep away
All the cares of the day
Cast out shadows, cast out wrong
Make the circle safe and strong

Lay the broom aside and step into the circle. Spend a few
moments in contemplation of the sacredness of the
space around you. Then step toward the altar
to bless the salt and water.

BLESSING THE WATER

Place the bowl of water on the pentacle.
Take your athame and slowly lower it
into the water until its tip touches the
bottom. Visualize an electric blue
light flowing from the blade and say:

I bless this water in the names of the God and the
Goddess. Let there be no harm contained within,
only goodness that shall aid my work tonight.

BLESSING THE SALT

Place the bowl of salt on the pentacle and again lower the athame into it, visualizing a blue light dancing through it. Say:

I bless this salt in the names of the God and the Goddess. Let there be no harm contained within, only goodness that shall aid my work tonight.

Pour the salt into the water and set aside for later.

DRAWING THE CIRCLE

Taking the sword or athame, stand facing the north, where the altar is. Hold the sword out straight and visualize a blue or white light coming from its tip. Walking deosil, "draw" the circle with the light, envisioning a protective wall or sphere growing around you. Make sure you include the whole of the altar and all the objects you will be using in the rest of the ritual within this protective boundary. As you draw the circle, say:

O circle of mystery, thou art constructed tonight by my will and by the will of the God and the Goddess. Sacred place that lies beyond time and space, neither of men nor of the gods, protect us as we perform our works and guard the power raised within. In the name of the God and the Goddess, I consecrate you and I bless you.

LEAVING THE CIRCLE

When the circle has been cast, it is best not to break its boundary by moving outside its circumference. If it is necessary to leave or to enter, a "doorway" should be opened in the northwest by using your athame to "draw" a small piece of the circle in a widdershins (counterclockwise) direction and then laying the athame at the threshold. To close the door, use the athame to redraw that piece of the circle in a deosil direction.

THE QUARTERS

A magic circle is divided into four quarters by the cardinal points north, south, east, and west. Each point is associated with an element, an elemental, and in some traditions, a watchtower.

The elements represent the forces of nature that make up the material world of the cosmos. Elementals are the creatures of the elements, and if left unrestrained, can sometimes cause trouble. The elementals are controlled by higher spiritual beings called the lords of the watchtowers; their individual names vary from tradition to tradition.

After casting a magic circle, you need to invoke the elements and their associated elementals. Some (although not all) Wiccan traditions then summon the watchtowers in order to control the elementals. Each tradition has its own way of summoning these powers, sometimes drawing from other magical paths and cultures, such as Nordic, Egyptian, or Judeo-Christian (Kabbalistic). There is no right or wrong way to do it; the important thing is that it works for you.

To begin, pick up the bell from the altar and ring it three times (the number of the Goddess), pause for a few seconds, then ring it another two times (the number of the God).

THE QUARTERS AND THEIR ASSOCIATIONS				
QUARTER	**ELEMENT**	**ELEMENTAL**	**WATCHTOWER LORD**	**MAGICAL TOOL**
North	Earth	Gnomes	Boreas	Pentacle
East	Air	Sylphs	Eurus	Wand
South	Fire	Salamanders	Notus	Sword
West	Water	Undines	Zephyrus	Chalice

EARTH

With the pentacle, walk deosil around the circle, holding it up at each quarter and saying:

I call upon the element of earth to bless this circle. May it protect us with its grounding force as we perform our works tonight.

WATER

Take the bowl of salted water and walk around as before, splashing drops of the water around the circle's edge. As you do so, say:

I call upon the element of water to bless this circle. May it grant us inner sight as we perform our works tonight.

INVOKING THE ELEMENTS

AIR

Carry the smoking censer from the altar deosil around the circle. If others are present, waft the incense under their noses. Say:

I call upon the element of air to bless this circle. May it take our prayers to the God and Goddess as we perform our works tonight.

FIRE

Pick up one of the two altar candles and carry it deosil around the circle, holding it up at each quarter and saying:

I call upon the element of fire to bless this circle. May it grant us inspiration and passion as we perform our works tonight.

SUMMONING THE WATCHTOWERS

Whether or not you summon the watchtowers, the guardians of the four directions, is up to you. Some Witches find that summoning the elements is sufficient; others like to include a greater amount of ritual. The guardians are summoned by drawing special invoking pentagrams in the air using the athame. Note that the north watchtower is summoned first (and banished last when the ritual or ceremony is complete). This is because the north is also associated with the God and Goddess.

↑ NORTH WATCHTOWER

Stand in the north of the circle and draw the earth-invoking pentagram, saying:

> Boreas, lord of the north and the watchtowers of the north, with this sign we do summon, stir, and call thee forth. Be thou a protection and a guardian of the northern portals.

→→ EAST WATCHTOWER

Standing in the east, draw the air-invoking pentagram and say:

> Eurus, lord of the east and the watchtowers of the east, with this sign we do summon, stir, and call thee forth. Be thou a protection and a guardian of the eastern portals.

↓ SOUTH WATCHTOWER

Stand in the south and draw the fire-invoking pentagram, saying:

> Notus, lord of the south and the watchtowers of the south, with this sign we do summon, stir, and call thee forth. Be thou a protection and a guardian of the southern portals.

←← WEST WATCHTOWER

Standing in the west, draw the water-invoking pentagram and say:

> Zephyrus, lord of the west and the watchtowers of the west, with this sign we do summon, stir, and call thee forth. Be thou a protection and a guardian of the western portals.

EARTH-INVOKING
NORTH

WATER-INVOKING
WEST

AIR-INVOKING
EAST

FIRE-INVOKING
SOUTH

BLESSINGS AND CONSECRATIONS

Any objects that are to be used in the forthcoming rite or spell should be consecrated at this point—the ingredients for making a bag charm or talisman, for example. Similarly, cakes and wine, which are consumed at all Wiccan rituals, need to be blessed.

Some Wiccans bless and consume the food and drink at this point, after invoking the elements and summoning the watchtowers; others do so at the end of the ritual. You can choose whichever time you prefer, or that seems most suitable for the ritual you are performing. If a long ritual is being conducted, it is best to bless the wine at the beginning and save some for a "wine break" later on. If you do not consecrate enough, you can always bless more during the ritual. Any leftover wine and cakes, consecrated or not, can be drunk after the ceremony has ended.

CONSECRATING WORKING OBJECTS

Pass the object over the flame of an altar candle, saying:

> I consecrate thee by the power of fire.
> In the name of the God and Goddess,
> let all evil spirits be burned out so
> that this may become a tool of my will.

At the same time, visualize the flame's energy surrounding and filling the object with its power. Repeat the above chant, inserting the element name air, while passing the object over the censer of burning incense. Then do the same for water, passing the object over the dish of salted water, and finally for earth, passing the object over the pentacle.

CONSECRATING MAGICAL TOOLS

New magical tools need to be consecrated before use. This can be done in the same way as you would consecrate the other working objects for your rituals, after casting the magic circle (see left). However, if you are working in a solitary situation and do not have any previously consecrated tools with which to cast the circle or symbolize the elements, you can bless new tools without casting a circle first and simply recite the invocations alone. Remember, Wicca is an individualistic, nondogmatic religion, and your intent is more important than anything else.

BLESSING THE WINE

Most Wiccans choose red wine because its color represents blood, the sacred substance of life. However, cider or beer would be good alternatives during harvest, and mead in the summer. Milk could also be used, or apple or grape juice. If working alone, fill the chalice with wine and stand it on the pentacle on the altar. If both a male and female Witch are present, the male should hold the chalice, kneeling, and the woman stand above him. Dip your athame into the wine, saying:

As the athame is to the male and the chalice is to the female, so conjoined they bring blessedness. I bless this wine, athame to chalice, man to woman, heaven to earth. Blessed be.

BLESSING THE SABBAT CAKES

Sabbat cakes, also known as moon cakes, are eaten at all rituals and festivals, and represent the bounty of the earth and the body of the Goddess. Those who eat them are therefore sharing in earth's gifts. Place the platter of cakes on the pentacle on top of the altar, then perform an earth-invoking pentagram (see page 59) over them with the wand, saying:

Earth mother, we thank you for this food and ask that all who eat of it shall have health and happiness, wisdom and love, full storehouses and many blessings. So mote it be.

At the end of the pentagram, press the wand on top of the cakes in an act of blessing. You can then eat a cake. If more than one person is present, pass the platter in a deosil direction around the circle.

RECIPE FOR SABBAT CAKES

1 tbsp (15ml) honey
2½ cups plain
(all-purpose) flour
1 tsp (5ml) baking powder
½ tsp (2.5ml) salt
1¼ cups oatmeal
½ cup brown sugar
1 tbsp (15ml) wine
A few drops of vanilla essence
Pinch of cinnamon

Mix the dry ingredients together, then add the honey, wine, and enough water to make a dough. Roll out on a floured board and cut into crescent moon shapes with the edge of a cup. Place on a greased baking (cookie) tray and cook in a preheated oven at 350°F (180°C/gas mark 4) for 15 minutes or until light brown.

PRAYERS AND CHANTING

Now that the magic circle is ready, you need to invite the God and Goddess to join the rite, and then chant a rune of power to raise the energy within the circle in readiness for the remaining rituals, spells, and seasonal festivities that to be performed.

PRAYERS TO THE GODDESS AND GOD

Here are some sample prayers to the Goddess and God, though you can create your own if you prefer. Note that the God and Goddess are invited, never summoned; it would not be polite to do so.

PRAYER TO THE GODDESS

Lo, Goddess, gentle lady
We come to you, hearts afire with your love
Burning with your wisdom
O thou who art named Isis, Cerridwen
Ishtar, Brigid, Hathor, Demeter, Danu
I call to thee to come into our presence tonight
Descend to us on a shaft of silver moonlight
Appear to us in a dream or a whisper
Tell us how we might best serve thee
And listen to our needs
Mighty mother of us all, both living and dead
Come now unto us as we call to you
For thou art welcome here with us
And unto you we shall do honor

Right: The green man—representations of whom date back to ancient times—is one of the God's identities. With his face surrounded by leaves, he symbolizes harmony with nature.

PRAYER TO THE GOD

Lord of many names, master of disguises
Cernunnos, king of the wild places
Hear our prayers
And come dancing
Through the tall grass
Across concrete deserts
And lend your spirit of fierce joy
To our celebrations and rituals
My lord of plenty and all that is good
We ask you here to witness our needs and our actions
And fill our cups to overflowing that we may worship you evermore

RUNES OF POWER

Unlike the runes used further on in this book for spellcraft, runes of power are not written symbols but chants designed to raise power during a ritual. The power raised is known as the cone of power because it resembles a Witch's hat for those sensitive enough to see it. Covens chant runes of power while moving in a deosil direction around the magic circle, hand in hand. A solitary Witch could adapt the ritual by dancing up the power around the circle by herself.

CIRCLING RUNE

Circle around, hand in hand
We call the powers of this land
By the cord that binds us all
By all that flies and swims and walks
By earth and sea
By moon and sun
By life and light
It shall be done
By rock and tree
And ancient lore.
The cone of power
Is strengthened more
Earth and water
Air and fire
Bring to us
What we desire
The dance is danced, the song is sung
What we will, it shall be done
What we will, it shall be done

(repeat last line until high priestess calls "stop")

DRAWING DOWN THE MOON

This ceremony is used by some covens to draw down the power of the Goddess upon a designated priestess as a blessing, The woman chosen is usually experienced in the ways of Wicca. It is conducted at rituals when the moon is either waxing or full, and is performed prior to the rites and spells described in the following two chapters.

Although traditionally performed by a man and a woman, this ritual can easily be adapted for solo use. To begin, the woman stands in the pose of the Goddess (arms out to the side and bent up at the elbows), while the man kneels before her. He then uses the wand to trace a symbol representing the Goddess upon the body of the priestess, starting at her right breast, moving to her left breast, and then to her womb, then repeating all three again, and ending at her right breast. As he does this, the priest says:

I invoke thee, O mighty mother,
ancient ancestress of the gods,
measurer of time and weaver of
worlds. O thou who can make the
forest barren and the desert bloom.
O most ancient of powers, on you
we call to descend upon the body
of thy servant and priestess
standing here before you.

The priestess then recites an invocation.
"The Charge," written by Doreen Valiente,
is often used; an alternative is given here.

INVOCATION

Children of the earth, gather around, hear my words
Children of the stars, listen to me, hearken to me
Those who would be awakened from slumber
To the joys and pangs of life in all its colors
This is my message
From old, you know me; you have always known me
I am the kick inside the womb, I am the blood that flows so red
I am the star-encrusted night, I am the ebb and flow of the tide
I am the warp and I am the weft, I weave the tapestry of all life
The flowers dance in my name
Go forth into the world and sing my song
Let joy be heard in all places
Even the darkest stairwell or the barrenest desert
Let the truth that is inside you guide you onward
Let your heart be open both to give and receive in grace
Know that you are one with all living things
And that all living things are one with you
Love all the children of the earth
Take care of them for they are all my children
Keep safe my beasts and my birds, my fields and forests
Rivers and seas, high mountains and low valleys
For you are the caretakers of the future time
You are the guardians of tomorrow
When tomorrow comes, you will be able to stand proud
You were true to your inner destiny, your soul's path
Feel the spark of unique divinity within you
Cherish it and honor its sacred flame
Heed my words, children of earth
I am the great mother and you know me of old
Everywhere and yet nowhere, within and without
I bless you all with my love

CLOSING THE CIRCLE

After the ritual, it is essential that the spirits are thanked and dismissed, and the circle dismantled. This is good magical "hygiene," for if traces of magic are left, strange things can start to happen.

Stand in the east of the circle with your athame outstretched and perform the air-banishing pentagram, saying:

> Eurus, lord of the east and the watchtowers of the east, thank you for your presence and protection tonight. As this circle is closed and you return to your realms, I bid you a kind farewell.

Repeat for the south (Notus, fire) and west (Zephyrus, water), using the appropriate lord's name and banishing pentagram. Then do the same for the north, using the earth-banishing pentagram and saying:

> Boreas, lord of the north and the watchtowers of the north, O great God and gentle Goddess, I thank you for your presence tonight. As this circle is closed and you return to your realms, I bid you a kind farewell.

Ring the bell ten times (the number of the mundane world), blow out the candles, dismantle the circle, and return the tools to their storage space. Now "ground" yourself.

GROUNDING

Rituals and visualizations can leave you feeling spaced out or with too much magical energy. To carry on in either condition is potentially harmful. To ground yourself, sit on the floor and connect yourself to the earth via your palms, feet, and bottom. Feel the energy of the earth below you—it is strong, slow, and steady. Pull that energy into your body through your contact points, and feel it working its way around your whole system. Eventually, it flows back into the earth again, taking any excess energy, tiredness, or negativity with it. When you feel it is done, thank the earth and have something to eat and drink (another good grounder).

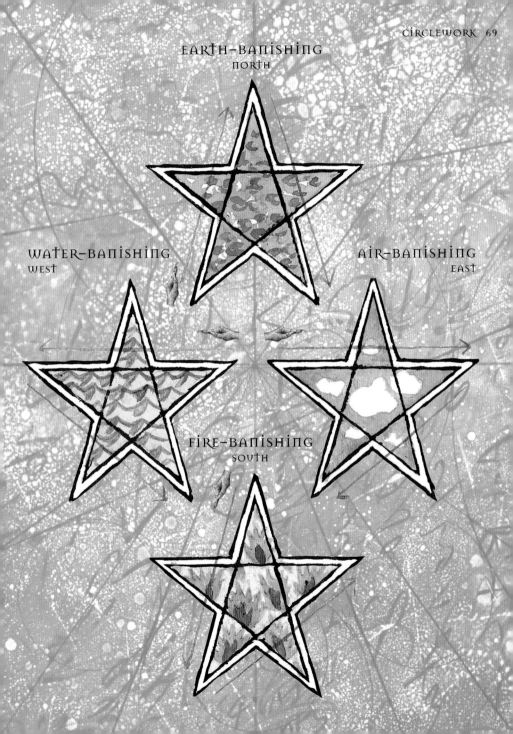

EARTH-BANISHING
NORTH

WATER-BANISHING
WEST

AIR-BANISHING
EAST

FIRE-BANISHING
SOUTH

FESTIVALS AND RITES OF PASSAGE

Celebrating special times of the year is part of the
Wiccan way of life. They are marked with rituals,
feasting, and sometimes singing, dancing, and games.
The eight seasonal festivals are known as sabbats.
Festivities are also held to celebrate the full moon and
various rites of passage. If these do not take place
at the time of a sabbat, they are called esbats.

THE EIGHT SABBATS

There are eight sabbats, or seasonal festivals, which together make up the "wheel of the year." Four mark the solar phases of the year (two solstices and two equinoxes), four are Celtic in origin. The dates given here are generally accepted, though some covens calculate them more precisely according to planetary positions. Most Wiccans celebrate on the nearest weekend for convenience.

WINTER SOLSTICE

Wiccans celebrate the rebirth of the sun at the Winter Solstice. It marks the time when the hours of darkness are at their greatest and daylight at its minimum. However, it is also the turning point, as after this date, the daylight hours begin to lengthen again.

IMBOLC

Imbolc is the celebration of the goddess's recovery from giving birth to the sun at the Winter Solstice. This is the season when sheep come into milk ("imbolc" means "to milk"), echoing the goddess giving nurture to her newborn son/sun. It is a time for celebrating the goddess as a bringer of fertility.

SPRING EQUINOX

The hours of light and dark are equal at this time of the year, with the light beginning to gain. If the sun was a baby at Imbolc, at the spring equinox he is a youth, becoming armed and ready for manhood.

BELTANE

The Celtic fire festival of Beltane is perhaps the one most associated with fertility. This is the time when the young god mates with the goddess of the land in a sacred union that begets the fruits of the earth.

SUMMER SOLSTICE

This is a celebration of the longest day, when the powers of light are at their strongest. However, this festival is also tinged with sadness, because from now on, the hours of darkness will grow. The sun now is a middle-aged man, a mighty warrior who has just reached his peak.

LUGHNASADH

Lughnasadh marks the time when the crops are ripening and will soon be cut. Fruit is swelling upon the trees and the land is about to slip into the richness of fall. At this time the sun god is nearing the end of his reign.

FALL EQUINOX

This is the culmination of the harvest season, and a time when day and night, dark and light, are equal. Within the life of man, fall equinox represents maturity, a time of rest after life's labors, and indeed it is a time of rest within the year—between the harvest being gathered in and the long dark ahead.

SAMHAIN

In the Celtic world, Samhain marked the end of one year and the beginning of another. It is a time for settling affairs in preparation for the period of darkness and renewal ahead.

SPRING EQUINOX
MARCH 21

BELTANE
APRIL 30

SUMMER SOLSTICE
JUNE 22

IMBOLC
FEBRUARY 2

LUGHNASADH
AUGUST 1

WINTER SOLSTICE
DECEMBER 22

SAMHAIN
OCTOBER 31

FALL EQUINOX
SEPTEMBER 21

Above: These dates apply to the northern hemisphere. If you live in the southern hemisphere, the dates are reversed so that the wheel of the year matches the seasonal cycle, with Winter Solstice on June 22 and so on. However, many Wiccans only reverse the dates of the solstices and equinoxes, and celebrate the four Celtic festivals, such as Samhain (Halloween), on their traditional northern hemisphere dates; others prefer not to reverse any of them.

WINTER SOLSTICE

Alternative name: Yule

Two themes dominate the Winter Solstice festival—the birth of the sun, and the battle between darkness and light. This concept of light and dark should not be misinterpreted as good versus evil—light and dark complement each other and form a balance that provides for our needs. The battle is often represented as a fight between the Oak King (light) and the Holly King (dark), with the Oak King triumphant.

THE TIME OF MISRULE

The period between Samhain and Imbolc is known as the time of misrule, and although the sun is reborn at the Winter Solstice, he does not have enough strength to create order in the world until Imbolc. Nevertheless, Winter Solstice is a time of inspiration and looking forward to the rest of the year, a time of beginnings, jollity, and of course, a little bit of mischief.

WINTER SOLSTICE RITE

Snuff out all candles except for one on the altar (to see by). Place the cauldron in the south of the circle with an unlit candle inside (a tealight is ideal). Light the candle, then face west and say:

Queen of heaven, great mother of all things
It is the time to bring forth your son
Unveil the dawning light of promise
Give to us the hope of harvest
Take away our sorrows
As you give birth to the new day

Turn to face the east, arms wide open, and say:

Lord of the sun, lord of light
Return again to warm this land
To ripen our crops
To brighten our children's faces
Come and chase away the darkness
Banish the cold that chills our bones
And makes our hearts ache
Return, O lord of light
Your people are waiting

WINTER SOLSTICE CELEBRATIONS

★ If you have a fireplace, burn a Yule log (traditionally oak). Place it on the fire before the circle is cast.
★ Decorate the circle with holly, ivy, mistletoe, and other evergreens.
★ Appropriate colors are white, red, and green.
★ Write your goals or resolutions for the coming year on a piece of paper and keep it safe.
★ Reenact the battle of the Oak King and Holly King with wooden swords or staves (the Oak King should win).

IMBOLC

Alternative names: Candlemas, Lupercalia, Feast of Brighid
Imbolc is celebrated as a sign that winter is nearly over and spring is on the way. It is also a festival of light, and often the priestess presiding over the ceremony wears a crown of lights (fairy-lights rather than

candles) to represent this bright aspect of the goddess. The most common form of the goddess invoked at Imbolc is the Celtic deity Brighid (pronounced Breed), associated with childbirth, fertility, healing, fire, craftsmen, poets, and the hearth.

LUPERCALIA

During the Roman festival of Lupercalia, the feast of Pan, priests ran naked through the streets, striking everyone with goatskin thongs, especially married women. This was very much a festival of purification and cleansing, albeit a cheerful and bawdy one. However, the scandalized Christian church took a different view and the festival was banned in CE 492.

Gentle goddess
Give of your milk of goodness
That we may all be nourished
Bring us your fire of inspiration
So that we can create wonder
Within us and around us
Warm our hearts with your love
Teach us with your wisdom
So that we know your value
And the value of nurture
Lady of the spring
Whenever you are near
Flowers grow where you tread
And trees burst into bud
Brighid, mother of us all
Come now, we beg you
And bring to us your hope
Brighid is come
Brighid is welcome

IMBOLC RITE

Stand in the north, facing the altar. Lay a Brighid doll (a simple doll shape fashioned from oat straw or reeds) in a straw-filled crib, and place the wand alongside (to represent a phallus). Say the chant written on the left.

Leave the crib overnight by whatever you regard as the household hearth. Afterward, put the wand away with the rest of your magic tools, then wrap Brighid and her bed inside a cloth, and put them in a safe place within the house.

IMBOLC CELEBRATIONS

★ Substitute milk for the sacred red wine.
★ Decorate the circle with fresh greenery and colourful spring flowers.
★ Appropriate colors are white, silver, and gold.
★ Compose a poem and read it aloud during the ceremony, or recite a favorite one.

SPRING EQUINOX

Alternative names: Eostre, vernal equinox, Ostara
The main symbols for this festival are the egg and
the hare. The hare (now the Easter bunny), a creature
of the moon goddess, was thought to lay eggs at this
time. The Mediterranean festival of Eostre (later
Christianized to Easter) may have had its beginnings
in the ancient cults of the goddesses Ishtar and
Astarte, and would have contained fertility themes
of sacred marriage. Interestingly, in modern Wicca,
these themes tend to come at the next festival,
Beltane. One explanation is that spring comes
much earlier in the Mediterranean.

Above: A queen offering vases to the
goddess Hathor, the Egyptian equivalent
of Astarte and Ishtar.

SPRING EQUINOX RITE

Standing before
the altar, raise
the wand in
your right hand
and proclaim:

By the bursting buds of springtime
Come unbounded, unhindered
By the bright daffodil
And the drooping snowdrop
Come racing through the green
By the sap that rises in the tree
By the lust that rises in the loins
We call for your presence
O lord of the forests
We pray you to descend now
And enter among us

Perform an earth-invoking pentagram
(see page 59), then hold the sword aloft
in your left hand and say:

Lord of light, I give you this sword
That you may be armed
Against despair and cruelty
To all that we love
Go forth in strength and truth
Go forth in the name of the lady

SPRING EQUINOX CELEBRATIONS

★ Decorate
hard-boiled
eggs and hold
an Easter-
egg hunt.
★ Lay daffodils and other spring
flowers around the altar.
★ Appropriate colors are
red, yellow, and gold.
★ Bless and eat eggs
(including chocolate eggs)
during the festivities.

BELTANE

Alternative name: May Eve

The one festival more or less left alone by the Christians, Beltane lives on in popular traditions in the phallic shape of the maypole. The ribbons that twine around it during the maypole dance (pictured on the right) are seen as female, and so their union is actually a symbolic mating of the God with the Goddess. In ancient times, cattle were driven between two bonfires to ensure their fertility, and human sexuality was celebrated in "greenwood marriages" and "staying up to watch the sun rise." Today, things have been toned down a little: there are usually no cattle, the bonfires are a little smaller, and any "sacred marriages" generally take place between established couples in private.

BELTANE RITE

Add 3 drops of cinnamon oil to some almond oil, and place this on the altar. Put two unlit candles in small, cauldron-like vessels and place them in the center of the circle, a yard (meter) apart. If you are working outside, two small bonfires, or Bel-fires, may be prepared instead. Walk around them three times in a deosil direction, declaring:

Summer is coming, the Bel-fires shall be lit
Time for celebration, time to make merry
Time to be of ourselves and no one else
Time to bless and time to be blessed
So light the fires, summer is coming
Light the fires, summer is coming
Light the fires, summer is coming
Light the fires, that we should know love

Light the two candles or fires, then step between them, starting in the south and finishing at the altar. Anoint yourself with the oil on your forehead, over the heart, and just above the pubic area, saying:

Let the mind be free
Let the heart be free
Let the body be free

GREENWOOD MARRIAGES

At Beltane, a man and woman could go off into the woods and commit to each other in a greenwood marriage. Its "legality" lasted for a year and a day, when it could be dissolved by either party. The term has also been applied to any sexual liaisons between men and women (even if married to other people) on May Eve. For that night, no one had the right to judge or punish them, and any resulting children were deemed legitimate "children of the greenwood."

BELTANE CELEBRATIONS

★ Decorate the circle with hawthorn, blackthorn, black oak, or water oak.
★ Appropriate colors are green and white.
★ Play forfeit games.
★ Elect a May queen.

SUMMER SOLSTICE

Alternative name: Midsummer, Coamhain, Litha

The Summer Solstice celebrates the longest day of the year, and is marked by the battle of the Holly King (light) with the Oak King (dark), in which the Holly King is victorious. It was extremely important to the ancient Celts; many stone circles, including Stonehenge (pictured above), are aligned with the rising midsummer sun. It is believed that on midsummer night, the gates between this world and the world of faeries are opened, and the faery folk can come and go at will. Welcome them in, if you wish, but beware, for they have a reputation for mischief. Whatever you do, never eat any of their food, for it is said that anyone who eats of their fare will be their servant forever.

SUMMER SOLSTICE CELEBRATIONS

★ Decorate the circle with solar images, sunflowers, and sweet-scented summer flowers and herbs.

★ Appropriate colors are gold and yellow.

★ Wear daisy-chain crowns and necklaces.

★ Reenact the battle of the Holly King and the Oak King (the Holly King wins).

SUMMER SOLSTICE RITE

Facing north, draw
the earth-invoking
pentagram (see page 59)
and say:

Above: On midsummer night, faeries can come to the earthly realm at will.

Lord of the heavens, bringer of light
You who are known by the names of
Lugh, Balin, and Cernunnos
We ask you to attend this celebration in all your glory
On this, your day of strength
Give us your fire, bless this earth
That we may not go hungry
That we may not go thirsty
That we shall have shelter in the cold
And health throughout the dark months
Lord of the solar disk
Nourish our souls
And as the days grow darker
Keep your promise to return

In return for the God's blessing, promise to do
something for the earth—perhaps recycling waste
or tidying local litter.

LUGHNASADH

Alternative name: Lammas

The name of the festival (pronounced loo-nus-uh) comes from the Druidic festival of Lugh, the Celtic sun god. In some ancient traditions, this is the festival in which the sun god dies, usually in a ritual sacrifice of some sort. To commemorate him, the ancient peoples of Britain and Ireland held processions, feasts, and athletic games in his honor. It makes more sense if we see this as the beginning of the hunt for Lugh—the chase that will end in the fatal cut that marks his death at the fall equinox, the end of the harvest. With the first cutting of the grain, this was also traditionally a feast of bread.

LUGHNASADH RITE

Bless a loaf of bread (preferably homemade) in the same way as you would bless sabbat cakes and place it in the center of the circle. Holding an ear of corn (wheat) in your hand, say:

Behold, the first cutting of the corn
And the baking of the first loaf
It is the bread of life
It is the seed of life
Let us give thanks for the start of the harvest
Let us pray for food for all

Break the bread into pieces, and holding the corn in one hand and a piece of bread in the other, meditate on the process for one to become the other. When you have finished, eat the bread, saving one piece to be crumbled outside as an offering to the earth.

LUGHNASADH CELEBRATIONS

★ Make corn dollies and eat bread-based foods such as pizza.
★ Decorate the circle with stems of grain plants, such as wheat, barley, and oats.
★ Appropriate colors are honey-yellow and orange.
★ Collect flower seeds and store them in little earthenware pots, or replant them in the ground after the ceremony.
★ Play team games to honor the games of Lugh.

Right: Celtic Druids held festivals to celebrate Lughnasadh in ancient times in honor of their sun god, Lugh.

FALL EQUINOX

Alternative name: Mabon

Fall equinox marks the end of the hunt for Lugh, who hides in the last sheaf of corn until it, too, is cut down. However, his spirit still lives on, hidden in the seed grain. At fall equinox, Wiccans give thanks for all they have received during the year—both the bounty of the crops and personal achievements—and make preparations to get through the days of darkness.

THE ELEUSINIAN MYSTERIES

In ancient Greece, this was the time for the "Eleusinian Mysteries," a secret and symbolic set of rituals that drew thousands of initiates and pilgrims each year. Although the content of these rituals was never passed on, it is understood that they had something to do with the grain harvest and the hidden seed within.

FALL EQUINOX CELEBRATIONS

★ Decorate the circle with harvest fruits and vegetables, and fall leaves.
★ Substitute the sacred red wine with beer or cider.
★ Appropriate colors are russets and orange.
★ Sit around a bonfire roasting marshmallows and chestnuts, and tell stories about the harvest.

FALL EQUINOX RITE

Place fruits and vegetables of the season in the middle of the circle, then recite the following before feasting on the produce:

Great mother of the earth
Lord of the hunt and the wild places
We give thanks tonight for the bounty before us
We give thanks for the fruits from the trees
The plants and roots from the earth
And for the animals in the field
We give thanks for food in our bellies
For clean, pure water
And for being able to draw breath each morning
We give thanks for a sheltering roof
Four strong walls
And a warm hearth
We give thanks for the family that gave us life
For the friends who surround us with love
And for the children who bring us hope
We give thanks for those who have taught us
Those who have sacrificed life and freedom for us
And those who inspire us to better things
For all that is our life, we give thanks
And what we have received from the gods
We must return to those around us

SAMHAIN

Alternative names: Halloween, All Hallows Eve

Samhain (pronounced sow-een) is perhaps the festival most associated with Witches and magic. Marking the end of one year and the beginning of the next, ancient Celtic tribes held assemblies during which disputes were settled and marriages arranged. On a supernatural level, it is the time when the veil between the worlds is at its thinnest and spirits, elementals, and divine beings are able to walk upon the earth unsummoned. It was considered that the night of Samhain was a time when faery folk and other elemental beings interfered with the affairs of humans, causing havoc across the land. Within Wicca, Samhain is a time for honoring ancestors with prayer and feasting, and time is usually given over to divination.

SAMHAIN RITE

Stand in the circle facing west and say:

God of the dark months
Lord of the far realms
We come to thee on this night of shadows
To seek your boon
Lift the veil between the worlds
And let our ancestors and loved ones
Come forth in peace
Let them feast with us and commune with us
Before returning to the Summerlands
O great teacher
Teach us the cycle of death and rebirth
So that we are unafraid to journey there
Show us what love there is beyond death

Draw the earth-invoking pentagram (see page 59), then close your eyes and remember those who have gone before. This can be loved ones or those who paved the way for modern Wicca.

SAMHAIN CELEBRATIONS

★ Place mementoes of departed loved ones on the altar or in the west of the circle.
★ Appropriate colors are black and brown.
★ Decorate the circle with pumpkins with carved faces, tell ghost stories, and eat pumpkin pie.
★ Use the cauldron for apple-bobbing competitions.
★ Leave a cup of wine and a sabbat cake outside the door as a token feast for the spirits.

Right: The Hansel and Gretel fairytale features the type of Witch popularly associated with Halloween. This could not be farther from the truth.

OTHER CELEBRATIONS

In addition to celebrating the seasons, Wiccans perform rituals to honor the full moon, work magic, and mark various rites of passage through life. Such rituals sometimes form part of the sabbat festivities, but if held at other times of the year, the celebration as a whole is called an esbat.

ESBATS

Rituals held to celebrate the full moon are called esbats. There are thirteen full moons in a year, and in some traditions, each one has a name, such as harvest moon. At these times, the moon aspect of the Goddess is honored and magic or divinations may be performed. However, esbats are not just limited to the full moon; the name is also used to describe the holding of any ritual that is not a sabbat. This means that if you cast a circle to perform spellwork, whether it is in the waxing, waning, or new phase of the moon, it could be termed an esbat.

WICCANING OR NAMING

This is the Wiccan equivalent to the baptism of a child, and different traditions Wiccan children at different ages. Usually the child is not committed to a spiritual lifetime of being a Wiccan; they are merely put under the protection of the God and Goddess until they can reach an age where they can decide their spiritual path for themselves. Within the ceremony, the child is presented to the God and Goddess as well as the elements and the watchtowers. A number of guardians (equivalent of godparents) are appointed to watch over the child. During or after the ceremony, the child is presented with gifts to aid it on its journey into adulthood.

PUBERTY RITES

Many native peoples observe the passing of their children into adulthood, and this is becoming increasingly common within Wicca. The form of the ritual is fluid and should be light in nature—more of a celebration than a ceremony. It could mark a girl's first period or a boy reaching the age of 13 or 14 (a bit like a bar mitzvah). However, one important point should be stressed; no matter how eager the parents, a child should never be pushed into such a ceremony. Doing this could result in resentment and psychological damage.

Left: A Wiccan conducting a ritual at Glastonbury Tor, England. Glastonbury is the mythical site of King Arthur's Camelot and a popular location for magical festivities.

Initiation

Most covens hold initiation ceremonies to welcome newcomers into the Wiccan priesthood. Each coven will have its own version of the initiation ceremony. However, if you are a solitary, you can self-initiate using a ritual such as the one described here.

Prepare a bottle of anointing oil by adding 3 drops of cinnamon oil to some almond oil. Place it on the altar together with a length of red thread. You will also need an initiate's cord (red if you are female, blue if you are male; see page 38). Cast a circle and call upon the four quarters (see pages 50–59), then kneel before the altar and say:

> At this place within the sacred circle and at this time
> The time of the gods
> I have come before you to dedicate myself to your service
> O most ancient God
> O bountiful Goddess of the earth and the heavens
> I know myself as your child, newly awakened
> I recognize my own divinity and the divinity of all life around me
> Guide my path, teach me new learnings
> Surround me with your love as I make my first steps in your names
> Let me always be welcome to sit at the warmth of your hearth fires
> In perfect love and perfect trust, so mote it be

Anoint the area over the third eye (middle of the forehead), saying:

> Bless my mind, that it shall always be open to the truth

Next, anoint the spot over your heart, saying:

> Bless my heart, that it shall always show compassion
> And love for all around me

Finally, anoint just above your pubic area, saying:

> Bless my body, that it shall serve you faithfully

Sit quietly in contemplation for ten minutes or so, making sure that you are comfortable and warm enough (it may be a good idea to place a blanket in the circle before the ceremony). Sit in complete silence and empty your mind as much as possible. If you find that thoughts do creep in, gently move them aside and then continue. After a while, you may feel a deep sense of peace and love, or you may receive a vision. If so, remember to write it down after the ritual and keep it safe.

When you feel ready, slowly come out of the meditative state and kneel again before the altar. It is now time to make your dedication. Take the thread and tie eight knots in it, as equidistant as possible. As you tie the knots, say the following:

> This first knot is for knowledge
> This second knot is for truth
> This third knot is for strength within
> This fourth knot is for love
> This fifth knot is for honor
> This sixth knot is for reverence
> This seventh knot is for magical will
> This eighth knot is for dedication to the service of the old ones
> All these things do I bring to the Craft
> I dedicate my will to the furthering of my knowledge
> And I pledge my service unto others
> Eight words the Wiccan Rede fulfill
> An' it harm none, do what ye will

Drink a toast to the God and Goddess, then tie the cord of initiation around your waist. If you wish, sit in quiet meditation for a short while longer, then close the circle (see pages 68–69). Keep the knotted thread safe, perhaps attached to the cord around your waist, until you feel that the effects of the initiation ritual have become manifest within you.

HANDFASTING

Handfasting is the term given to a Wiccan or pagan marriage. In the United States, handfasting is recognized legally as long as the necessary paperwork, such as a marriage license and blood tests, is carried out. In other countries, such as Britain, it is not legally recognized.

Handfastings are generally carried out by a high priestess and/or high priest. Some advertise their services in pagan and New Age publications, so even solitaries should be able to find someone to carry out a handfasting for them if they so desire. Most handfastings are beautiful occasions, with vows exchanged and the clasped hands of the bride and groom bound with a silver cord to symbolize their togetherness. Afterward, there is much feasting and merriment. Handfastings are usually performed at Beltane, but they can be conducted at most times of the year. The exception is the period between Samhain and Imbolc, when the energies are not in tune with such ceremonies. Handfasting is seen as a new beginning, so it is best carried out during a new or waxing moon.

FUNERALS

Civil funerals can usually be arranged without orthodox religious overtones, so many Wiccans are content with this. However, things are beginning to change in this area, and funeral ceremonies carried out by Wiccan priests and priestesses do happen. Methods of burial are also becoming more environmentally conscious. The subject of arranging Wiccan "crossing over" is a wide topic and best covered by those who have studied it closely. Starhawk's *The Pagan Book of Living and Dying* covers most aspects of death and bereavement.

Right: A Wiccan handfasting is a beautiful occasion when a bride and groom exchange vows.

SPELLWORK

When people think of Witchcraft, they think of
spells. Wiccans use spellcrafting to help and to heal,
but never to harm. In this chapter you will find a few
simple ways to bring a little magic into your life;
when you become more experienced and confident,
you can devise some spells of your own.

THE POWER
OF SPELLS

Spells use force of will to create the right circumstances for what you want to happen. The most important tool for this is your imagination. You will need to visualize your desired outcome, and pour your whole will into that visualization (see pages 46–47). This energy then creates a channel for the spell to work.

Above and far right: Books of Shadows describe spells, rituals, and the tools used to perform them.

Spellwork usually requires working tools—candles, herbs, and so on. These will not make a spell work, but they do provide a focus for your will, as well as add a little of their own energies. You must also bear in mind that the universe is not an inert place waiting for your spell to come along and flow through it; it is alive with other energies and currents. Some of these will be stronger than yours and may be operating in the opposite direction. If this is the case, the effect of your magic will be negated and you will have to try again another time.

Spells can be performed as part of larger rituals, or you can simply cast a circle, invoke the quarters, pray to the God and Goddess, and consecrate the items needed for the spell. Then perform the spell and close the circle. (See circlework, pages 40–69.)

SPELLCASTING ETHICS

Wiccans do not use magic to harm others, and there is a tradition that any spell will come back on its sender to the power of three. Even apparently "good" spells may be unethical. For example, you should not cast a love spell to enchant a particular person, since you would be using magic to influence someone against his or her will. It is better to cast a spell to draw the right person to you, whoever he or she may be. Similarly, you should not cast a healing spell without the person's consent, and it is important to make sure that he or she continues with medical treatment. Remember that most spells need a way of materializing in this world, whether that is via medicine (for healing), playing a lottery (for money), or socializing (to find love). Magic requires that we do a little pragmatic work, too.

TABLES OF CORRESPONDENCE

These tables are guidelines for achieving the optimum conditions for working different types of spells—the best day on which to perform a spell, the most appropriate aspects of the god and goddess to invoke, and so on. However, remember that the most important thing for a spell's success is your intent.

PROTECTION

Elements	All, especially fire
Colors	White, silver
Day	Sunday
Plants	Acacia, garlic, agrimony, clove, basil, hazel, bay, holly, cinquefoil
Stones	Amber, stones with natural holes, hematite, yellow fluorite
Incense	Frankincense, rosemary
Goddesses	Artemis, Sekhmet, Isis
Gods	Thor, Herne, Cernunnos
Sigil	

HEALING

Elements	All
Colors	Blue, orange, white
Days	Sunday, Monday
Plants	Herbs that heal the physical body (consult a herbal)
Stones	Quartz, emerald, jade
Incense	Frankincense, eucalyptus, sandalwood
Goddesses	Hygeia, Isis, Cerridwen, Brighid
Gods	Apollo, Asclepius, Diancecht
Sigils	

LOVE

Element	Water
Colors	Pink, rose, orange
Day	Friday
Plants	Rose, jasmine, lavender, myrtle, honeysuckle, vervain
Stones	Rose quartz, emerald
Incense	Sandalwood, jasmine, rose, patchouli, musk
Goddesses	Venus, Aphrodite, Isis, Ishtar
Gods	Eros, Cernunnos, Pan
Sigils	

CREATIVITY

Elements	All
Colors	All, especially yellows and oranges
Day	Wednesday
Plants	Lavender, valerian, honeysuckle, vervain
Stones	Citrine, amethyst
Incense	Citrus, bay
Goddesses	Brighid, Athena, Cerridwen
Gods	Apollo, Hermes, Thoth
Sigil	

STRENGTH

Element	Earth
Color	Red
Days	Sunday, Tuesday
Plants	St. John's wort, oak, bay, pennyroyal, plantain, thistle
Stones	Bloodstone, agate, garnet, lapis lazuli, tiger's eye
Incense	Frankincense, bay, cinnamon, lotus
Goddesses	Macha, Scathach, Athena
Gods	Zeus, Hercules, the Dagda, Lugh
Sigil	

ABUNDANCE

Element	Earth
Colors	Green, purple, gold, silver
Days	Thursday, Sunday
Plants	Basil, buckwheat, allspice, rice, cinnamon, mint, vervain, dill, dock, wheat, goldenrod, goldenseal, woodruff
Stones	Aventurine, green jade, garnet
Incense	Cedar, mint, vervain
Goddesses	Demeter, Cerridwen, Hera, Danu
Gods	The Dagda, Cernunnos, Zeus
Sigil	

FERTILITY

Elements	Earth, water
Colors	Green, red
Days	Monday, Sunday
Plants	Rice, grain plants, fig, geranium, grape, sunflower, poppy, pomegranate, hawthorn, mistletoe
Stones	Pearl, kunzite, emerald
Incense	Patchouli, musk, vervain, pine
Goddesses	Isis, Astarte, Ishtar, Rhiannon, Brighid, Demeter, Freya
Gods	Pan, Osiris, Cernunnos, Zeus
Sigil	

BANISHING

Element	Earth
Color	Black
Day	Saturday
Plants	Birch, garlic, frankincense, elder, juniper, rosemary, rue, yarrow, mullein
Stones	All black stones
Incense	Frankincense, rosemary
Goddesses	Macha, Scathach, Sekhmet
Gods	Herne, the Dagda, Cernunnos, Thor
Sigil	

CAПDLE ṁAGiC

Candle magic is one of the most common ways of performing a spell, and relies on visualization and concentration for it to work. The candles are chosen and consecrated as symbols of what it is you are working for. In other words, they become representative of your wish, making candle magic a form of sympathetic magic.

PREPARiПG AПD DRESSiПG CAПDLES

Inscribe candles with any sigils that seem appropriate using the white-handled knife. If a spell requires you to "dress" the candle with annointing oil, place a dab of oil on your middle finger, then run your finger along the candle from the middle upward, and then from the middle downward, concentrating your will on the outcome of your spell all the time.

CAПDLE ṁAGiC TO EASE GRiEF

Many people find comfort from burning a candle during painful times in their lives, such as after having lost a loved one. According to Wiccan beliefs, death is only a temporary parting, and you will meet with your loved one again in the Summerlands.

Set up a personal altar where you can be alone and undisturbed. Place a picture of the loved one on the altar, together with some flowers, an image of the Goddess or God or both, and the candle. You do not need to consecrate or dress the candle unless you really want to, nor do you have to cast a magic circle.

Whenever you are in need of comfort (and there is no time limit on this), go to the altar, light the candle, and sit quietly, watching the flame. After a while, you may want to communicate with the loved one, or pray to the God and Goddess to grant him or her a safe passage and rest in the Summerlands. Do not be afraid to cry or feel angry; it is all part of the healing process. Eventually you will need the candle less and less, but of course you may have to burn several before your raw grieving is over.

YOU WiLL ПEED

Photograph of loved one

Flowers

Image of Goddess and/or God

Blue or white candle

CANDLE MAGIC TO ATTRACT LOVE

This spell is aimed at creating the right magical atmosphere for you to meet that special person. It should be performed every day for a couple of weeks, starting on a Friday as near the new moon as possible.

YOU WILL NEED

2 or 3 drops rose essential oil

1 tbsp (15ml) almond oil

2 red or pink candles

2 candleholders

Red or pink ribbon

Add the rose oil to the almond oil and dress the candles with it. As you dress the first candle, visualize yourself happy and in love with a person you have yet to meet, saying:

> I anoint this candle and name it for myself.
> It shall represent me in all matters of the heart.

Take the other candle and dress it, visualizing the unknown person possessing all you could love and desire in a partner. Say:

> I name this candle for he/she who is my future,
> my heart's desire. It shall represent him/her in
> all matters of the heart.

Set the candles in the candleholders and place them on the altar about 14 inches (35cm) apart. Tie one end of the ribbon to the base of each candleholder. Light the wicks, and as they burn, visualize yourself meeting this other person, becoming friends, and eventually lovers. After about ten minutes, move the candles about 1 inch (2.5cm) closer to each other. Do this by turning the candles slightly, so that the ribbon wraps itself around the candleholders as they move closer. As you turn the candles, say:

As the flames near and unite, so shall love between us ignite.

Blow out the candles. Every night until the full moon, cast a small circle of protection around yourself and perform the visualization again. Turn the candles a little each night, moving them closer and wrapping more of the ribbon around them (make sure the ribbon never gets too close to the flames). On the night of the full moon, bring the candles together so that they are touching. Repeat the words and the visualization, but this time remove the ribbon before you light the wicks and let the candles burn down completely. Keep the ribbon and any leftover wax in a special place, such as a spell box or under your pillow, until your goal has been achieved.

CANDLE MAGIC TO CREATE ABUNDANCE

Cast this spell for increased prosperity, but bear in mind that you must create a channel for it to reach you, such as playing a lottery or entering a competition. If possible, perform this spell on the day of a new moon.

YOU WILL NEED

Salt

3 drops peppermint essential oil

1 tbsp (15ml) almond oil

1 gold candle

2 green candles

2 purple or pink candles

5 candleholders

About 40 coins

Green cloth

Sprinkle a circle of salt on the ground, then sprinkle the shape of a pentagram inside it so that the points touch the circle. Add the peppermint oil to the almond oil, and use the mixture to dress the candles. As you do so, visualize receiving money, perhaps in the form of a large check arriving in the mail. Set the candles in their holders and place one at each point of the pentagram, with the gold candle at the top, the green candles next to the gold, and the purple or pink candles at the base. Carefully place a coin under each candle, making sure that the candles remain stable and will not topple over when lit. In the center of the candles, arrange the remaining coins along the arms of the pentagram. The pentagram shape is significant as it is the symbol of earth, the element of material riches. Keep visualizing receiving money while you are doing this.

When you are ready, and the picture of the outcome is strong in your mind, light the candles and say:

O great God, O lovely Goddess
I light these candles to bring me wealth
I ask not out of greed, but out of need
I ask you to grant me my wish
I ask you to bless me with what I need

Spend another ten minutes in contemplation, then leave the candles to burn down completely. At the end, gather up the remnants of wax and the coins, wrap them in a green cloth, and bury them in the earth.

TALISMANS AND RUNES

Talismans are spells that have been cast into an object that you can then carry around with you for optimum effect. Runic magic uses symbols from ancient languages and magical traditions so that a spell may be written down. Runic talismans can be made by decorating an object with appropriate runic letters.

TALISMANIC STONES AND OBJECTS

A simple talisman can be created using a special stone and consecrating it to your purpose (see the tables of correspondence on pages 100–101). Pieces of jewelry may also be used—the eye of Horus is a symbol of protection, the Egyptian ankh is symbolic of life, and the pentagram represents psychic protection. The list of symbols is endless, so it is best to study books that cover talismans in depth.

Another option is to etch an appropriate runic symbol into a piece of metal or wood.

Above: The first archeological evidence of runic scripts dates from the 3rd century AD. This detail from a 7th-century Anglo-Saxon casket features runic lettering above and below a hunting scene.

Left: Popular talismans include runestones, ankhs, pentagrams, and eyes of Horus.

RUПES

 FEOH Wealth, property, financial gain, status, security

 UR Physical strength or skill, masculinity, determination

 THORN Protection, defense, caution, patience

 AS Authority, knowledge, creativity, divine protection

 RAD Change, movement, progress, friendship

 KEN Warmth, celebration, love, success, regeneration

 GYFU Good fortune, new opportunities, partnership

 WYN Balance, luck, joy, contentment

 HAGAL Caution, surprises, disruption

 NYD Self-preservation, patience, constraint

IS Frozen emotions, patience, standstill

 GER Renewal, replenishment, future growth, gradual change

 **EOH** Flexibility, determination, steadfastness, protection

PEORTH Mystery, the not-yet-known, psychic links

 EOLHS Creativity, artistry, culture, increased talents

SYGEL Wholeness, life force, rest, recovery

 TIR Victory through energy and heroism, passion

 BEORC Growth, fertility, beginnings, good news

 EOW Travel, change, newcomers, excitement

 MAN Male authority, unity, steady progress

 LAGU Female intuition, fertility, creativity, productivity

 ING Fertility, family, good results, good news

DAEG Clarity, success, improvement, moving onward

 ETHEL Inheritance, the home, money matters

TALISMAN FOR PERSONAL PROTECTION

This talisman can be used to provide protection from all kinds of harm, and from any evil intent that another person may feel toward you.

YOU WILL NEED

Small, round mirror
Orange candle
Candleholder
Cloth, preferably white or silver

Place the mirror on the altar so that it catches the light of the candle. Point your athame at the mirror and say:

By this sacred blade, I charge you with protection. Turn back all evil, reflect back all negative thoughts, blind with light all those who would cause harm to me. May you be a shield, may you be a protector from this time forward. In the name of the God and Goddess, so mote it be.

Charge the mirror with energy from your athame by imagining an electric blue light flowing from the knife into the mirror. After the ceremony, wrap the mirror in a cloth, and if possible, carry it with you. If not, stand it on a windowsill, facing out into the world.

Runic magic to grant a wish

By writing your wish on a piece of paper, you can encourage it to come true. Always use red ink because red is the color of blood and life, so it helps to bring the spell to life.

You will need

Plain piece of paper

Pen containing red ink

Focus your attention on your desired goal, and write down one or more runic symbols that best represent your wish (see page 109). Sit quietly for a few minutes in front of your altar, then charge the paper with the power of the four elements. To do this, pass it over the candle flame (do not set it alight), then pass it through the incense smoke, then sprinkle it with salted water. Finally place it on the pentacle and say:

By flame, I charge this spell with life, that my will shall burn through the universe. By air, I breathe power into my words, so that they are carried by the wind to the edges of eternity. With water, I give birth to my desires, so that they flow to the sea of truth. By earth, my wish is materialized on this plane, so that I can reap what I have sown.

Keep the paper for a month, then burn it. If your wish has not been granted by that time, it is not meant to happen.

BAG CHARMS

These are little handmade bags, sewn from cloth of an appropriate color and filled with items such as herbs. They act in a similar way to talismans, and should either be carried with you or kept in a safe place.

BAG CHARM FOR A DESIRED JOB

YOU WILL NEED

Green or purple fabric

Herbal mixture

Silver coin or object to represent the job

Carry this bag charm with you, especially to any interviews, to help you get the job you desire. When you have done so, burn the sachet and remember to thank the God and Goddess for their help.

Make a little cloth bag and fill it with herbs such as cinnamon, cinquefoil, and honeysuckle. Place a coin or item that represents the job into the bag and sew up the open end or close it with a drawstring. You may also wish to sew a rune or sigil for success onto the bag. Sit quietly while holding the bag and visualize what you wish for, sending energy into the spell. When you have done this, pass the bag over the flame of an altar candle, saying:

Element of fire, I ask that you bless and consecrate this spell. Lend your energy that I may achieve my goal.

Pass the bag through the incense smoke on the altar, saying:

Element of air, I ask that you bless and consecrate this spell. Lend your powers so that I may be seen as suitable for this job.

Sprinkle the bag with salt water and say:

Element of water, I ask that you bless and consecrate this spell.

Lend your powers so that a channel may be opened up whereby I can come to this job.

Place the bag upon the pentacle and say:

Element of earth, I ask that you bless and consecrate this spell. Lend your powers that this job shall be mine. This job shall be mine. This job shall be mine.

Carry on repeating the last sentence while focusing on the outcome. When you feel that enough is enough, say three times:

The job is in the bag.

BAG CHARM TO ATTRACT LOVE

Use this rite to create a bag charm that will make you receptive to love. Keep the sachet with you at all times—place it under your pillow at night—until your true love appears.

YOU WILL NEED

Pink fabric, preferably velvet or satin

7 types of herbs

Pink ribbon

Sew a little bag from pink fabric and assemble seven types of dried or fresh herbs associated with love, such as rose, jasmine, lavender, myrtle, honeysuckle, vervain, and mistletoe. Place them on the pentacle on the altar and say:

> I bless these children of nature that they might aid me in finding the man/woman whose heart fits my heart and whose soul fits my soul. May they bring him/her to me across the wide spaces, may they draw us so that we may be eye to eye, heart to heart, body to body, and spirit to spirit. This is my wish, so mote it be.

Put the herbs into the bag and fasten it with the ribbon using seven knots (seven is the number associated with love). Sit quietly for a few minutes and visualize meeting someone whom you could love and who could love you back. See yourself as happy and full of self-confidence. When you feel you have put enough energy into the spell, pass the bag over the top of an altar candle, saying:

> Fire, bless this spell and bring me passion.

Pass it through the incense smoke and say:

> Air, bless this spell and bring me the art of communication.

Sprinkle it with salted water and say:

> Water, bless this spell and grant me a love as deep as the ocean.

Place it on the pentacle and say:

> Earth, bless this spell and bring this love into being.

Once your wish has been fulfilled, bury the sachet and plant an herb associated with love on top of it so that you can watch your love grow.

POPPETS

A poppet is a small, handmade doll that represents a living person. To make one, draw a gingerbread man shape on a doubled piece of fabric, allowing for seams. Cut it out, place the material right sides together, and sew, leaving a small gap in one side. Turn it right side out and fill with herbs or batting, then sew the gap closed. If you wish, embroider features on the doll. Poppets can also be made from wax or modeling clay, and some Wiccans use a photograph instead.

A HEALING POPPET

YOU WILL NEED

Poppet filled with healing herbs (consult a good herbal)

Although you can use a poppet to represent yourself if you are sick, it is more usual to perform this spell for someone else. However, you must always remember to get his or her permission before doing so.

Sprinkle a little salt water over the poppet, saying:

> Creature of magic, made by hand, I charge you into life. You are no longer mere materials but flesh and blood. I name you (name of person to be healed). You are his/her representative in this world and all others.

Holding the poppet gently, breathe life into it, at the same time visualizing the sick person healed again. Hold this picture for as long as possible, sending healing energy into the doll. When you have finished, keep the doll safe on the altar or in a special spell box.

When the healing has taken effect and the doll is no longer needed, deactivate it by sprinkling salt water over the doll and saying:

> Creature of magic, made by hand, your job is done. I take away your name of (person's name) and break the link. You are no longer charged with life. You are once again mere materials, a thing with no name. You have no name, you have no name, and you are no one.

Finally, immerse the doll fully in salt water to cleanse it, then dismantle it and carefully burn the components.

A BINDING POPPET

If a person has a hostile intent toward you, or is spreading malicious gossip about you, you may wish to use a binding spell to stop them from harming you further. This spell does not harm the recipient in any way, but it does stop them from making mischief for you. A binding spell should only be cast if the person is capable of inflicting real harm.

YOU WILL NEED

Poppet filled with batting
Black cord

Sprinkle the poppet with salt water and say:

Creature of magic, made by hand, I charge you into life.
You are no longer mere materials, but flesh and blood.
I name you (person to be bound). What you see, she/he will
see; what you hear, she/he will hear; what you feel, she/he
will feel. You are her/him in this world and all others.

Breathe life into the poppet, visualizing the person. Take the black cord and slowly bind it around the poppet. If the person is spreading gossip, you may wish to bind the mouth in particular. Say:

Hear my will, you are bound
By sun and moon, you are bound
By rock and water, you are bound
By fire and wind, you are bound
To do no more harm
Do no more harm
No more harm
No more harm
No more harm
You are bound
In the names of the God and Goddess

At the end of the ceremony, take the poppet out of the house, toward the north, and bury it under a heavy rock. Leave it there for as long as you wish. However, if the threat is no longer present and you wish to dismantle the poppet, use the routine described in the healing spell on page 116.

GENERAL SPELLS

Here are a few general spells that are easy to perform. They do not require you to make any special objects, or figure out appropriate colors and symbols, but they are just as effective as more complicated spells.

Above: Venus of Willendorf, a Stone Age carving of the earth mother.

YOU WILL NEED

Large black or gray pebble

GETTING RID OF ANGER

This simple visualization spell uses the power of the color black to absorb negative energies.

Sprinkle the pebble with a little salt water to cleanse it of previous influences, then sit with it in your hands. Think of what is troubling

you or making you angry, and feel the emotions flowing from your body into the pebble. See it filling up with all your problems, taking the negative feelings away from you. After the ceremony has finished, dig a hole and throw the pebble in. Ask the earth to take away your anger and problems, and thank her before filling in the hole. If you prefer, take the pebble to a river or lake and throw it as far as you can into the water.

GETTING RID OF NEGATIVITY

YOU WILL NEED

New piece of paper

Pen containing red ink

This spell is often carried out at Samhain, the end of the Celtic year, so that you can enter the new year in a more positive frame of mind.

Write down what you wish to be rid of in yourself. Make it quite specific and be honest. Burn the piece of paper either over a candle or in a fire, but make sure you do so safely—paper can often flare up more than you expect. As it burns, visualize the old habits changing into ones that you would prefer and say:

Creature of fire, burn away the old and the unwanted, and bring the new, the fresh, the clean, and the healthy into my life. Let it take hold within me from this point forward.

HOUSE PROTECTION SPELL

Feeling safe within your own home is vital for health and happiness; perform this spell to conjure a protective shield that will help keep your home free from negative vibrations.

Visualize the house surrounded by a circle of golden or electric blue light. This will extend your "working circle" so that you can move around the entire house to perform the spell. Walk around the house sprinkling the salt water wherever there is an opening—doors, windows, hearths, and so on. Say at each opening:

> With this salt and water, I seal this house against evil.

Next take a candle around the house, repeating in every room:

> Spirit of fire, cleanse all malignancy from this place and bless the hearth with your warmth that friends may always gather.

Take the incense around the house, blowing it into every corner.

> Spirit of air, blow away all unclean energies from this place.

Finally, take around the pentacle, saying:

> Spirit of earth, bless this house with strong foundations, strong walls and a strong roof, that it may protect those who live within.

If at any time you feel the need to strengthen this protection, visualize the house surrounded once again by a golden light, a psychic shield that no harm can pierce. If you have visitors who leave behind negative energy, cleanse the house by walking around it again with some incense, making sure that you fill every room with its scent. Then open the windows for an hour or so.

GLOSSARY

ATHAME A black-handled knife used by Witches to cast circles and control spirits.

BOOK OF SHADOWS The traditional working book of a Witch that contains all his or her rituals, spells, and training guidelines.

CARDINAL POINTS The four directions: north, south, east, and west.

CENSER A container used to hold burning incense. Represents the element air.

CHALICE Sacred cup that symbolizes the female, and the Goddess within the circle. Represents the element water.

THE CHARGE Chant used by many Wiccans within the drawing down the moon ritual.

CIRCLE A sacred space, constructed and consecrated by ritual, in which rites, ceremonies, and magic are carried out. Considered to be "between the worlds."

COVEN An established group of Witches who meet regularly to perform rituals and celebrate seasonal rites. Usually run by a high priestess and a high priest.

DEGREE A level of achievement gained within certain Wiccan traditions. Usually initiatory and at the discretion of the coven leaders.

DEOSIL Sunwise or clockwise. This is the direction in which most movement takes place within a circle.

ELEMENTALS Creatures associated with the elements that may be summoned into the circle. The elementals are: gnomes (earth), sylphs (air), undines (water), and salamanders (fire).

ELEMENTS Forces of nature—earth, air, water, and fire.

EQUINOXES The quarter points of the year when the hours of light and dark are equal. These occur in spring and fall, and are

celebrated by Wiccan festivals known as sabbats.

ESBATS A ceremony that is not at the time of a sabbat. Usually, but not necessarily, held on the night of a full moon.

FESTIVALS The collective name given for the sabbats, the eight occasions when the wheel of the year is celebrated.

GOD The male aspect of the creative, divine force that is present in every aspect of the universe. The God can take many forms and have many names, but he is always in balance with, and complementary to, the Goddess.

GODDESS The female aspect of the creative, divine force that is present in every aspect of the universe. The Goddess can take many forms and have many names, but she is always in balance with, and complementary to, the God. Most often she is seen as having a triple aspect—maiden, mother, and crone.

GROUNDING
Neutralizing excess
magical energy by letting
it flow into the earth.

HANDFASTING
The Wiccan and pagan
ritual of marriage.

INITIATION A ritual
induction into Wicca,
given in a special
ceremony. Mandatory in
some traditions, but not in
others. Spiritual initiation
is something different
and personal only to the
individual involved.

MUNDANE Something
that is material and
everyday—not magical.

OLD RELIGION
A phrase coined by the
author Margaret Murray
to describe Wicca. She
believed that she could
trace the roots of modern
Wicca in a straight line
back to early medieval
times. Many of her theories
have now been discounted,
but the term remains in use.

PENTAGRAM The five-
pointed star that has
become most associated

with Wicca and paganism.
It represents the four
elements ruled by spirit,
as well as being the symbol
for the element earth within
the circle. The magical
tool representing the
pentagram in the circle
is called the pentacle.

POPPET A small doll
usually made from fabric
and filled with herbs or
batting, that is used in
spells to represent a person.

QUARTERS The north,
south, east, and west
segments of the circle.

RUNE Either a magical
symbol or a chant used to
raise power within a circle.

SABBATS The eight
seasonal festivals that mark
the wheel of the year. They
comprise two equinoxes,
two solstices, and four
Celtic festivals.

SIGIL Magical symbol.

SKYCLAD Being naked.

SOLSTICES Points within
the year when either the
hours of light have reached
their greatest (Summer

Solstice) or the hours
of darkness are at their
longest (Winter Solstice).
They are two of the sabbats
celebrated by Witches.

SPELL A way of causing
magic to happen by force
of the will. Usually other
working tools and items are
involved, such as candles.

SUMMERLANDS
The place we go to when
we die so that our spirits
can rest before moving
on to the next life.

TALISMAN An object
that carries the power of a
spell. Most associated with
protection, luck, or love.

WATCHTOWERS Rulers
of the elemental energies
and quarters who give
protection during a ritual.

WICCANING A ceremony
for children asking the God
and Goddess to protect
them until maturity.

WIDDERSHINS To move
counterclockwise within
a circle (the opposite of
deosil). Usually associated
with banishing or chaotic
magic, it is not often used.

Ï∏DEX

RECOMMENDED READING

An ABC of Witchcraft, Doreen Valiente

The Book of Runes, Ralph Blum

Celtic Gods, Celtic Goddesses, R. J. Stewart

Complete Idiot's Guide to Wicca and Witchcraft, Denise Zimmermann, Katherine Gleason

Cunningham's Encyclopedia of Magical Herbs, Scott Cunningham

Diary of a Witch, Sybil Leek

Drawing Down the Moon, Margot Adler

Eight Sabbats for Witches, Stewart Farrar

The God of the Witches, Margaret Murray, Sampson Low (although many of the theories in this book have now been disproved, it still makes good reading)

The Greek Myths, Robert Graves

Lid Off the Cauldron, Patricia Crowther

Living Wicca: A Further Guide for the Solitary Practitioner, Scott Cunningham

Magical Rites from the Crystal Well, Ed Fitch

Moon Magic, Dion Fortune (a novel that has had great influence on ritual workings)

The Myth of the Goddess: Evolution of an Image, Jules Cashford, Anne Baring

Natural Magic, Doreen Valiente

The Pagan Book of Living and Dying, Starhawk

Practical Candleburning Rituals, Raymond Buckland

The Practice of Witchcraft Today, Robin Skelton

The Sea Priestess, Dion Fortune (an occult novel that has influenced many a ritual)

The Spiral Dance: A rebirth of the Ancient Religion of the Great Goddess, Starhawk

The Tree, Raymond Buckland

What Witches Do, Stewart Farrar

Wicca: A Guide for the Solitary Practitioner, Scott Cunningham

Wicca: The Old Religion in the New Age, Vivianne Crowley

Witchcraft for Tomorrow, Doreen Valiente

A Witch's Grimoire of Ancient Omens, Portents, Talismans, Amulets, and Charms, Gavin Frost

The Witch's Magical Handbook, Gavin Frost, Yvonne Frost

The Witches' Way, Janet Farrar

CREDITS

Quarto would like to thank and acknowledge the following for supplying pictures reproduced in this book:

Key: B = Bottom, T = Top, L = Left, R = Right

Ann Ronan Picture Library 6L, 13, 85, 120TL. **Corel** 23, 28R, 79TR, 82/83. **Fortean Picture Library** 7TL, 7TR, 16B (Kevin Carlyon), 17T (Kevin Carlyon), 25, 51 (Allen Kennedy), 83BL, 95 (Kevin Carlyon), 98L (Raymond Buckland), 108R. **Sally Griffyn** 7BR, 90. **Science Photo Library** 42BL. **Spectrum Colour Library** 81.

All other photographs and illustrations are the copyright of Quarto. While every effort has been made to credit contributors, we would like to apologize should there have been any omissions or errors.